# Musings on Life

*Peggy Vaughan*

Dialog Press
San Diego, CA

Copyright © 2008 Peggy Vaughan

All rights reserved. No part of this publication
may be reproduced, in whole or in part, in any form.

Cover Photo of Peggy by James Vaughan

ISBN 978-0936390239
Manufactured in the United States of America

Visit Peggy's Website: www.musingsonlife.com

To my Wonderful Granddaughters
With Love from Nana

# Table of Contents

Introduction .................................................................... 1

1. Lessons in Living ............................................... 3
   If I Could Live my Life Over
   Living in the Fast Lane
   Living in the Moment
   Living While Dying
   One More Year
   Never Really Prepared

2. Stages of Life ..................................................... 17
   Personal Life Changes
   Keeping up with Life's Changes
   Downsizing your Life
   Weddings—and Time
   Youthful Dreams
   The Rest of Your Life

3. On Being a Woman ........................................... 31
   Women of Courage
   Respecting Women's Choices
   'Working' Mothers
   Balancing Home and Work
   Dancing as Fast as I Can
   Spending Time Alone
   It's Not Easy Being a Woman

4. Love/Relationships ........................................... 49
   Marrying Young

Valentine's Day Thoughts
   The Power of a Kiss
   Sleep (the Cuddle Factor)
   Love, Sweet Love
   Lessons in Love
   Friends
   Love and Devotion

5. Family ................................................................................67
   Family Patterns
   Family Gatherings
   Family Keepsakes
   Mother's Day
   Special Memories
   Who You Gonna Call?
   Running with the Boys
   The Soccer Generation
   Children without Families
   Happy 100th Birthday!

6. Character and Integrity ......................................................87
   Character Assessment
   Trusting your Intuition
   The Power of Integrity
   Strengths and Weaknesses
   Your Net Worth
   My Quest for a Wii
   When Dreams Come True
   Pressure to be Perfect
   Winning and Losing
   Telling the Truth

7. Communication ................................................................109
   The Power of Words
   Parent—Child—Adult
   Ignoring the Elephant in the Room
   Debating vs. Discussing
   Everybody's Talking

8. Simple Pleasures ............................................................. 121
   It's the Little Things
   Seeking Happiness
   Music Makes me Happy
   Enjoying America's Pastime
   Dog Days of Summer
   Talking about the Weather
   Desperately Seeking Nature
   Vacation Time
   What do you Enjoy?

9. Health and Fitness .......................................................... 137
   Let's Get Physical
   Stress!
   Killer Headaches
   Getting a Good Night's Sleep
   Age is Relative
   The Common Cold—and Cancer
   Breast Cancer Awareness
   Living with Breast Cancer
   Minor Surgery
   What You Don't Know *Can* Hurt You
   Modern Medical Advances
   Losing my Mind

10. Learning/Education ....................................................... 161
    School Days
    How's Your Education?
    Public Education
    Graduation Day
    Lifelong Learning
    Bookaholics
    Awards that Matter

11. Technology ................................................................... 179
    Me and My Computer
    Internet Savvy
    Love/Hate Relationship

12. Freedom and Responsibility ............................................. 187
    Citizens of the World
    Soldiers Serving in Iraq
    "The War"
    Voting: a Right and a Responsibility
    Summons for Jury Duty
    Report on Jury Duty
    Political Awareness
    Remembering the Past
    Getting Along

13. Making a Difference ....................................................... 203
    Doing Good in the World
    Helping Others
    Giving and Receiving
    Patience and Persistence
    Help in Times of Crisis
    Pay it Forward
    Supporting those in Crisis
    Giving—Large and Small

14. The Big Picture .............................................................. 223
    Our Planet's Past
    Global Warming
    Nowhere to Hide
    Out of this World
    Where All Things Belong
    We're All in this Together
    The Whole World

# Introduction

*"If I tell many first-person stories in this book, it is not because I am obsessed with my own life or delude myself about its importance, but simply because it is the life I know best, and it provides all sorts of examples that I suspect are typical of most people's lives."*

—Douglas Hofstadter

This statement accurately reflects my feelings about the 'musings on life' that I share in this book. Although I begin most of the pieces with a reference to something from my own personal experience, I then broaden the focus to reflect on the larger issues involved and invite you to consider how they impact you.

I wrote these columns over a two-year period between May 2006 and May 2008. They're not presented here in the order in which they were written but are organized according to topics or themes—although I do note the month in which each article was written

I also tried to write about issues that are universally relevant or meaningful—because the underlying theme of the book is recognizing and acknowledging the many things that bind us all together as people.

It's my hope that these writings will serve as motivation or inspiration for each of you to take time to do your own 'musings on life.'

## Chapter 1: Lessons in Living

If I Could Live my Life Over
Living in the Fast Lane
Living in the Moment
Living While Dying
One More Year
Never Really Prepared

*Lessons in Living*

## If I Could Live my Life Over            December 2006

When we reflect on where we are in our lives, most of our musings focus on things about ourselves we'd like to change in order to be happier, healthier or more successful. Interestingly, the changes we'd like to make tend to be pretty much the same ones year after year.

We seem to think we've got unlimited time to do whatever we really want or need to do. Of course, we know better if we stop to think about it, but we seldom slow down enough to do this kind of serious contemplation about life.

Another reason we sometimes fail to take stock of our lives is that we simply don't want to focus on our own mortality. However, I find that doing that kind of specific focusing on the end of life allows me to feel much calmer about life on a day-to-day basis.

Every day is an opportunity to take charge of our lives and live in a way that prevents us from coming to the end with regret that we didn't fully live. So it's important to consciously focus on how you're living your life day to day. It's far better to do something now rather than wait until it may be too late—and wind up living your last days with regret.

Here's a piece that I hope will motivate you to think about what you'd do 'if you could live your life over.'

If I Could Live It Over
Author Unknown

*(This has been printed in a number of publications through the years, showing the author as 85-year-old Nadine Stair, Don Herold, 'anonymous' and others.)*

## MUSINGS ON LIFE

If I had to live my life over again,
I'd dare to make more mistakes next time.

I'd relax. I would limber up.
I would be sillier than I have been this trip.

I would take fewer things seriously.
I would take more chances. I would take more trips.

I would climb more mountains, swim more rivers.
I would eat more ice cream and less beans.

I would perhaps have more actual troubles,
but I'd have fewer imaginary ones.

You see, I'm one of those people who live seriously
and sanely, hour after hour, day after day.

Oh, I've had my moments. And if I had it to do over
again, I'd have more of them.

In fact, I'd try to have nothing else, just moments,
one after another, instead of living so many years
ahead of each day.

I've been one of those persons who never goes
anywhere without a thermometer, a hot water bottle,
a raincoat and a parachute.

If I had it to do again,
I would travel lighter than I have.

If I had to live my life over, I would start barefoot
earlier in the spring and stay that way later in the fall.

\* \* \* \* \* \* \* \* \*

*Lessons in Living*

## Living in the Fast Lane                         June 2007

> *"Life's so quick; life's so fast.*
> *At this rate will I last?*
> *How on earth will I stay sane?*
> *Living in the fast lane."*

These opening lines from the Simon Icke song "Living in the Fast Lane" reflect the way many of us feel these days. We find ourselves overscheduled and overstressed, rushing around multitasking our way through life. It seems that we might slow down as we get older, but I find I'm actually picking up speed—and it's not a good thing.

Everything I do feels almost like a race, beginning with the way my mind races most of the time. I've always walked fast and talked fast and been generally quick about everything I do, but there seems to be a new intensity these days. Not only am I concerned that I may be harming myself physically, but my hurried, harried state is not good for those around me either.

Recently we took a day off—away from home and computer—and went for a drive and a hike and just exploring places we hadn't seen before. I've often noticed that the only times I feel remotely mellow are when I'm outside my normal environment. And every time this happens, I vow to get out of my (self-imposed) routine more often.

In fact, it's foolish to push myself the way I do, especially since I have flexibility in the way I choose to use my time and energy; so I have no one to blame but myself. Others who have 9 to 5 jobs or are stay-at-home moms don't have as much choice. But all around me I see people who are pushing themselves more and more every day.

So I invite you to join me in committing to try harder to slow down and smell the roses. It's ironic that I use the words 'try harder'—since that's the same mindset that gets us stuck in this fast lane to begin with. But we do need to focus on the trade-offs in our quality of life (and probably in our effectiveness) by virtue of our fast-paced way of living.

Here are a few more lines from the song "Living in the Fast Lane:"

> "Peace of mind I have no more,
> Simple life has gone for sure.
> Always wanted, in constant demand.
> Mobile in car, mobile in hand."

The above verse refers to one of the issues most of us face—being constantly 'connected.' So one thing I've done is to give my cell phone number *only* to my immediate family. I hope each of you will consider what you can do to take a break from the fast lane—and bring a little more peace and calm into your life.

\* \* \* \* \* \* \* \* \*

**Living in the Moment**  May 2007

Most of us stay so busy that we miss out on a lot of life's basic pleasures. We could find much more enjoyment and satisfaction by being more fully aware of what's going on around us.

This kind of mindfulness has been described as 'living in the moment.' But it's important to clarify just what it means to live in the moment. It's *not* 'living it up' as if there's no tomorrow—the proverbial 'eat, drink and be merry, for tomorrow we may die' mentality.

## Lessons in Living

Living in the moment was best described by one of my favorite authors, Ted Rosenthal, who was 34 years old and dying of cancer when he wrote a book called "How Could I Not Be Among You?" He said: *"People misunderstand the whole notion of living FOR the moment versus living IN the moment. To live IN the moment...is being able to live life fully from moment to moment."*

Here's another of my favorite quotes, this one from Einstein: *"There is more to life than increasing its speed."* But as the pace of life grows increasingly rushed and hectic, it gets harder and harder to stay in the present moment.

When I think back on earlier times, especially in the South where I was born and raised, I realize that life *seemed* to be far less rushed. This is not nostalgia for the 'good old days'—since, frankly, I think the current period is the best yet. But we need to be thoughtful about using our time in ways that enhance our lives rather than cutting us off from being fully present and engaged in whatever we're doing at any given moment.

Personally, I have a tendency to live 'inside my head,' focusing on whatever I'm thinking about instead of being fully focused on what's happening around me. Also, most of us have developed an amazing ability to multitask—which can really take us out of the moment. And while we're supposedly getting a lot done, we also wind up missing a great deal of the meaning in our lives.

So it's an ongoing struggle to remind myself to slow down and experience the world around me. And I hope you'll pause in your busy schedules and assess whether you're racing through life (feeling out of control and captive to your 'to do' list)—or really living your life 'in the moment.'

MUSINGS ON LIFE

\* \* \* \* \* \* \* \* \*

## Living While Dying                October 2007

I recently watched the best speech I've ever heard by anyone on any subject, (and I've heard quite a lot of speeches in my life). Since I believe this is one of the most important speeches anyone can hear, I want to encourage everyone to enrich their lives by watching it as well.

The speech provides valuable information and perspective (about both living and dying) from a man named Randy Pausch. He's a 47-year old man with a wife and three children and a successful career as a professor and innovator in computer science, specializing in 'virtual reality.' He's also a man who's dying of incurable pancreatic cancer, having been told he has about 3 to 6 months of health before the final days.

Many people are uncomfortable in talking about death and dying, particularly their own death, and you may not feel comfortable listening to someone do so. But be assured that this speech will *not* be a 'downer.' Randy sets the tone early on by telling the audience, *"If I don't seem as depressed or morose as I should be, sorry to disappoint you."*

Actually, this is one of the few times he refers to his current plight—since the speech is not technically about dying, but about living. It's filled with wisdom about how to pursue your dreams—and filled with inspiration as well as humor. In fact, the most striking statement he made (which was evident in the way he conducted himself during the speech) was, *"I'm dying—and I'm having fun."* This may seem impossible, but if you watch him deliver this speech, you'll have no doubt he means it.

*Lessons in Living*

When you're fortunate enough to hear someone with this kind of attitude speaking candidly about dying, it's wise to pay attention—and to learn. Even though I've always been open in talking about death, focusing on both my own death and dealing with the deaths of others close to me, I learned a great deal from listening to what he had to say and how he said it.

If you'd like to know more about Randy Pausch, you can go to his website and find links to a Google video of the speech, a piece from his appearance on Good Morning, America, a Wall Street Journal article and other follow-up articles and videos.

ADDENDUM: July 25, 2008. This is the day that Randy Pausch had been preparing for—the day of his death. I continued to follow his progress and to be inspired by the way he handled this whole process. Just yesterday I purchased his book, "The Last Lecture"—which includes more than just the lecture itself. I highly recommend it as an ongoing reminder of the important 'lessons in living' it offers to all of us.

\* \* \* \* \* \* \* \* \*

**One More Year**                                    **December 2007**

We tend to think that each New Year is an opportunity to make a 'fresh start' and address whatever goals we've not yet reached in our lives. But our New Year's Resolutions rarely last beyond the first few days or weeks. So rather than thinking about making changes for a *year*, it might be better to take it one *day* at a time. If we can focus on our goals for one day, perhaps we can then do it for another day—and another.

I was prompted to think about the power of the one-day-at-a-time concept when I recently saw the movie based on Mitch

Albom's book, "For One More Day." (You may recall he's the author of the very popular "Tuesdays with Morrie.") This newest book asks the question, *"What would you do if you could spend one more day with a lost loved one?"*

As we enter a New Year, this might be a good place to start—although perhaps not focusing on what we *would* have done, but on what we can *now* do or say to our loved ones while they (and we) and still here.

Frankly, I live with this awareness almost all the time and try my best to keep my important relationships up to date. I periodically check this out by asking myself, "If you lost a loved one today, would you say, 'If only'..." Then if I feel something is missing, I take steps to correct it.

I can't take credit for thinking of the importance of this way of living. It came as a result of observing my parents, each of whom in their own way showed me by example.

For instance, my Daddy died suddenly at age 57 of a massive heart attack. He'd always told me how much he loved me and showed it through his actions throughout my life, and he made sure I was clear on that before he died. It turns out that although he had not been diagnosed with heart problems, he sensed that he wasn't well. He just hadn't been feeling right the previous few months, even declining to come for a visit during the holidays because of it.

Then just two days after Christmas (exactly 36 years ago today), he called me early in the morning. He said he just wanted to make sure I didn't worry about him. While he'd never been one to talk in a philosophical way, he went on to say that he'd had a good life and never wanted to linger in a hospital. And his last words were, *"I love you, little girl."* (Even though I was 35 years old at the time, he'd always called me his 'little girl.') Three hours later I got a call that he'd had a heart attack and died. As you can imagine, his call gave me great comfort in my time of grief and has continued to bring me comfort during all the years since that time.

My Mother also showed great love and caring for me in the way she protected me from many of the practical responsibilities of responding to a loved one's death. She'd been quite sick for many years and never expected to live as long as she did (until age 71, the age I am now). So, long before her death, she had personally made all the 'arrangements,' including choosing her coffin and pre-paying her burial expenses. She also left me precise written notes about pall bearers, who to contact, etc. It was one of the most thoughtful, loving things in the world to know that she was thinking of how to protect me until the very end.

I've tried to follow my parents' lead in the way I've made plans that will ease the burden on my children at the end of my life. I too have pre-planned the handling of my own death and dying process: having a living will, durable power of attorney, and signing up to donate my body to medical science through the Total Body Gift Act.

If you're much younger, you may think you have 'all the time in the world' to make your relationships with your loved ones all you want them to be. And you certainly may think there's no need to think about your own death at this stage of your life. But no one knows how long they have to live—or how long their loved ones will be around. So accepting this reality may be a good place to start in setting your goals for the coming year. However, as I said in the beginning, it's not as realistic to plan for a year at a time as to act on a day-by-day basis—so you never wind up having to wish for 'one more year.'

MUSINGS ON LIFE

\* \* \* \* \* \* \* \* \*

**Never Really Prepared**  February 2008

My husband's sister died last night—after a long illness. She had lung cancer and had struggled for many years and undergone many treatments, until there was nothing left to do but keep her 'comfortable.'

At times like this, all normal schedules and responsibilities fade while we stop and focus on family and love and connections and all that this means. I find myself reflecting on all the times like this in the past—when sudden news of the death of a loved one made the world stand still.

My first experience with loss like this was when my husband's father died just two months after we married when we were only 19 and he was only 47. This was a sudden, traumatic loss, and we were totally unprepared.

Then when I was 35 and my Daddy died suddenly at the age of 57, it was another loss for which I was completely unprepared. When my mother died at age 71, it was after many years of serious health problems and a prolonged dying process. However, when she died I learned that these circumstances don't change the fact that you're Never Really Prepared!

My only consolation in the loss of my parents was that in each case I had left nothing unsaid and felt as complete in my relationships with them as is reasonably possible. However, even without the added burden felt by those who live with regrets following the death of loved ones, I felt (and still feel) a profound sense of loss.

I must also acknowledge that in addition to the sense of loss, I also feel a closer connection to them than when they were alive. That's partly because love never dies—and because I feel that I now carry them in my heart so that they are always with me. So even death does not cut the ties that bind us to those we love.

Death is a part of life, albeit one of the most difficult parts, but dealing with death can help us focus on the importance of not wasting our lives in petty pursuits or on petty priorities. Life is a valuable gift for which we need to show appreciation every day, knowing that it ends for all of us at some point.

So I want to remind myself (and all of you) to focus on what's really important—living each day so that we're better prepared when faced with death, knowing that we will never be fully prepared.

## Chapter 2: Stages of Life

Personal Life Changes
Keeping up with Life's Changes
Downsizing your Life
Weddings—and Time
Youthful Dreams
The Rest of Your Life

*Stages of Life*

**Personal Life Changes**  June 2006

Making any major change in your life can create a period of adjustment—even when it's *chosen*. However, 'choosing' can make it somewhat easier to adjust to the change. While it's always hard to let go of one part of our lives and move on to the next, it's wonderful when it can happen at a time and in a way of our own choosing. In fact, this process of deliberately choosing our path is one James and I have tried to follow since 1970. Prior to that time, we pretty much went along with whatever was presented to us or 'just happened.'

But in 1970, James walked away from tenure as a college professor to do independent corporate consulting. At that same time our youngest child entered school, so I began working with him. During that first year we began developing a life-planning program to use in our consulting. But after a few years, we realized we weren't implementing some of the concepts in our own life.

So we decided it was time to take a careful look at our overall situation and make a conscious decision about the future. In 1972 we went through our own program as participants, working through the material we had developed. By the end of the weekend session, we knew it was time for some changes. So in 1973 (being guided by the priorities we had identified during the program), we moved to Hilton Head, SC, where we lived for eleven years while raising our kids. By 1984, they were grown and on their own, so we again made a detailed assessment of our life situation and made a decision to move to San Diego, CA.

A lot of people who knew about the various moves we made would say things like, "I wish I could do that." They seemed to think we had some special freedom or financial security that allowed us to make these changes. However, that's not the case at all. In fact, we paid a high financial price for each change, leaving us at this stage of our lives without a nest egg or resources for retirement.

But we had carefully assessed the pros and cons of our options and the trade-offs involved, then prioritized our preferences, made a decision and acted on it. It's that same process that has led us to make many other significant life changes, appreciating the past but always looking forward to what the future may hold.

\* \* \* \* \* \* \* \* \*

**Keeping up with Life's Changes**             **December 2007**

As we go through different stages of life, we may find that our priorities shift to suit the changes in our lifestyle. In fact, it can be difficult to keep up with these changes as we find that our habitual way of making decisions lags behind the way our priorities change.

For instance, one of the most dramatic examples of this in my own life took place back in 1973 when we finally built the house we had been wanting for quite awhile. We had moved to a new city the year before and during that time had made some changes in our lifestyle. However, our house design had been in our heads for many years, during a period when we did a lot of entertaining. Our lifestyle had included regularly hosting lots of parties, including very large parties a couple of times a year.

So in building our house, we created a large open area—where living room, dining room and kitchen all flowed together. The purpose of the design was specifically to accommodate the kinds of big gatherings we'd enjoyed for so

## Stages of Life

many years. However, we failed to take into account the fact that we were entering a new stage of our lives where entertaining took a big back seat to other activities. Most of our new social habits revolved around the change in climate where the warm weather allowed for lots of outdoor activities, whereas our earlier location had been in a much colder climate. Anyway, we lived in that house for eight years—and never had a party during that entire time! Actually, we did host the breakfast get-together for our daughter's senior class following their big school party. And it was quite nice to have such a large area to accommodate all the kids in one place. But clearly, the design of the house was not a wise decision—since it was based on an outdated lifestyle.

Certainly, the above example was not a serious problem, but there are times when failing to take into account our changing lifestyles can cause difficulties. This is never truer than when it comes to our health and fitness. Most of use carry around in our heads an image of ourselves based on outdated information. And if we're accustomed to behaving in a certain way, it can be difficult to shift to more appropriate ways of behaving as we age.

These outdated behaviors are most obvious when observing people (mostly women) who continue to dress and act in a very youth-oriented way that doesn't fit the reality of who they are at that stage of their lives—or when observing others (mostly men) who continue to behave as if they're 'jocks' who can still perform athletically in the way they did in their youth.

The resistance to some of these physical changes is because we tend to view them in terms of *loss*. But the reality is that whenever something is lost, there's also something to be gained—that is, if we're not distracted by trying to hold on to an outdated pattern. For instance, while age brings some physical diminishments, it can also bring a degree of maturity, judgment and wisdom that's only attainable through a lifetime of experiences.

So it's up to each of us to stay tuned in to the changes that are taking place in our lives—and determine to consider what may be the positive side to these changes. In the final analysis, it's a matter of deciding whether we want to view our lives in terms of whether the glass is half empty or half full.

\* \* \* \* \* \* \* \* \*

**Downsizing your Life**              **November 2006**

Corporate downsizing has become an all-too-common experience in recent years, causing a lot of distress for those employees who get downsized out of a job. But there are periods in our personal life where we voluntarily do our own downsizing. (Of course, there are also the sad times in later years when some people are forced to downsize in order to go into a nursing home or other assisted-living situation.) But *choosing* to downsize can be an exhilarating experience!

Like most couples, James and I spent our early years 'upsizing'—beginning with our initial housing that consisted of a bedroom, kitchen and shared bath on a college campus. For seven years (while James was in college and then graduate school), we lived in a variety of small apartments, including two years in a trailer.

After he graduated and we began having kids, we moved up to larger apartments and houses—finally buying our first home when the kids were pre-schoolers. About seven years later, we built a home and lived there while we raised the kids.

*Stages of Life*

After the youngest graduated from high school, we began our period of downsizing by selling our house and renting a condo. We've continued to live in apartments and condos in various cities over the past 25 years. And we've continued to downsize with every move.

We moved to our current apartment about three years ago, so my rule of thumb is that if we haven't used something (*really* used it) during this three-year period—out it goes. It's amazing how much stuff you hold on to that you're not using. And it's even more amazing to find stuff you didn't even remember you owned.

I thoroughly enjoy sorting through our 'stuff' and deciding what to give away, throw away, or sell. It feels like ridding myself of lots of weight and living the simpler life I've often longed for. I just wish I hadn't waited so long to begin this process.

It's especially satisfying to get down to the core of keeping only what I actually need or highly value. I've also been organizing all the family photos and keepsakes to pass on to our kids. I love the idea of doing this now and having it all in such wonderful order—rather than at the end of our lives when the kids might have to do it for us.

I do hope that my sharing will lead you to consider whether you might enjoy some personal downsizing as well.

\* \* \* \* \* \* \* \* \*

**Weddings—and Time**                              **September 2006**

My mind is on weddings today—because today is the 20th wedding anniversary of our daughter and son-in-law. As a little gift to them, I took the old VCR recording of their wedding and put it on DVD.

In fact, I made a couple of copies, and in the process I watched the tape a couple of times, leading me to recall aspects of that day that I'd forgotten. For instance, a dear friend of mine was driving quite a long distance to attend and got a little lost, arriving shortly after the wedding ceremony began. So it wasn't until I was being escorted out that I saw her near the back. I spontaneously reached over and gave her a kiss before proceeding with my exit. Seeing this again on the DVD brought back lots of good feelings.

There's no recording of the day I got married 51 years ago, but watching my daughter's wedding did lead me to recall my own wedding day. The most memorable aspect of my wedding was the fact that during the ceremony itself, I was transported to some kind of place of heightened awareness—where everything (every sight and sound) was clearer than I ever recall either before or since that time.

This recollection caused me to long for more of those times when I'm really aware of the moment. All too often, I (like most people today) rush around, thinking about what I need to do rather than whatever I *am* doing. We seem only to give our full attention to the special, significant events of our lives, but find it very difficult to really be 'present' for the everyday experiences.

So the impact of focusing on the weddings and recalling the events of those days led me to recommit to trying to live more 'in the moment' every day of my life. In fact, I may make a point to regularly listen to a song by James Taylor that captures this idea.

Here are a few of the lyrics to this song, titled, "The secret of life is enjoying the passing of time."

## Stages of Life

*"Now, the thing about time is that time isn't really real*
*It's just your point of view*
*How does it feel for you*
*Einstein said he could never understand it all*
*Planets spinning in space*
*The smile upon your face*
*Well, welcome to the human race."*

I particularly like these words because they reflect how time is so subjective in the way we individually experience it. I've always been interested in physics, particularly the study of time, but it still doesn't seem possible that it's been 20 years since my daughter's wedding—or 51 years since my own.

\* \* \* \* \* \* \* \* \*

**Youthful Dreams**                                          **February 2007**

I'm one of the millions of people who have followed the American Idol TV show over the years—although not as faithfully as when it first aired several years ago. I do recognize that part of the attraction of the show for me is the fact that I was very much like some of the wide-eyed young hopefuls who have a special talent and dream that they will someday be a big-time entertainer. (In fact, I was so pleased about this new platform for talented young people that I regularly referred to the first year's winner, Kelly Clarkson, as 'my Kelly.')

I've also taken great delight in the huge success of Jennifer Hudson, who didn't win the American Idol crown but who just won one of the biggest prizes of all, an Academy Award for her amazing performance in the movie "Dreamgirls." I saw the movie three times, and cried every time when she sang her big show-stopping number, "And I am Telling You."

However, in the midst of the excitement of such colossal success stories as Kelly's and Jennifer's, it's useful to remember that this kind of dream fulfillment is very rare. For every talented person (in any field) who succeeds in this way, there are many, many more who do *not*! So while it's fine to have youthful dreams, it's important that they be tempered by reality.

For instance, I was a child who had great dreams of a future as a singer. I was constantly singing when I was growing up. In fact, in my very small town in Mississippi (where everyone knew everyone else), I was considered the 'local girl singer.' I sang at weddings, funerals, school productions, Rotary Club and Lion's Club meetings, etc. I even received my first (very small) payment for singing when I was seven years old.

I can't recall a time while growing up when being a professional singer wasn't part of my dream for the future. But it was not to be. When I was a child, I didn't really have a chance (no money, no connections, no opportunity) to 'make it big.' But it's questionable that I could've made it in the entertainment business even if I'd gotten a break—because by the time I became an adult, I was not that special in terms of talent.

Today there are many outlets, including the phenomenal power of YouTube, where people can be noticed that otherwise might not have gotten the attention they deserve. In fact, one of my motivations for writing about this at this time is that just yesterday I saw an amazing performance on TV by a 20-year old 'unknown' named Von Smith. The show had found him on YouTube and decided to give him a shot on TV—and he 'knocked it out of the park.' (A star is born!)

## Stages of Life

If you look for him on YouTube, he not only does the song he did on TV (the Jennifer Hudson song from "Dreamgirls"), but also "Somewhere Over the Rainbow" and a number of others. And he's in the process of establishing his own website for those who want to follow what's sure to be an exciting fulfillment of his youthful dreams.

I also found it interesting to note that both Von and Jennifer had previously failed to succeed when they got their first big chance at stardom. While Jennifer failed to win American Idol, it turns out that Von also had failed to win when he appeared on the syndicated TV talent show, Star Search.

Personally, I have no lingering thoughts about whether I might have succeeded if I'd had such opportunities. I'm realistic enough to know that even that kind of exposure wouldn't necessarily have worked for me. As I said earlier, while I was exceptionally talented as a kid, I was *not* exceptional as an adult.

When I married, I gave up most of my early dreams of singing, only allowing myself a few excursions back into that world. I performed in a couple of college productions and briefly tried my luck at singing in New York when we were living in Connecticut. But these were half-hearted efforts, at best.

Almost everyone has some alternative scenario in their heads of how their lives might have worked out differently. But for many years I've been quite clear that even if I had succeeded in my youthful dreams, the downside of the life of many (most?) entertainers is a life I would not relish. So when the older and more experienced side of me looks realistically at the life I chose instead of pursuing that path, I think the decisions I made have worked out well.

Of course, sometimes we don't actually make *decisions* about our lives—when events take over and move us in different directions. In fact, many people wind up following paths in their lives that result from dealing with some kind of crisis or some other significant event. But even without such a catalyst, very few people stick with whatever career they chose when they were first starting out. Most people today have several different careers during their lifetime.

However, it's possible that there are ways of still enjoying some part of our dreams—even if they don't match the image we had when we were young. For instance, one of the most wonderful experiences of my life happened a couple of years ago when I participated with my three granddaughters in a musical put on by the local studio where they take dance lessons. The show involved both singing and dancing. (I actually enjoy dancing even more than singing these days). So aside from my personal enjoyment of performing on stage, the real joy was in doing it *with* my grandchildren. This was never anything I considered when engaged in my youthful dreams about performing, but it was an absolutely wonderful experience!

\* \* \* \* \* \* \* \* \*

### The Rest of Your Life                    August 2007

I find that just about any idea you might ever consider has been expressed at some point in a song. The focus of this column is no different in that there's a song title that perfectly captures the question I want to pose for your consideration: "What are you doing the rest of your life?" This is a classic (music by

## Stages of Life

Michel Legrand and lyrics by Alan and Marilyn Bergman) sung by Frank Sinatra and Barbra Streisand, among others.

The reason I'm thinking along these lines right now is that I just read an excellent book by Abigail Trafford titled "My Time: Making the Most of the Rest of Your Life." The 'my time' refers to the period between middle age and old age—a time when most people are finally able to focus on just how they want to use their time, rather than it being taken up with responsibilities for career and/or raising a family.

At a much earlier point in time, when life expectancy was much shorter, this 'my time' period didn't really exist. And then as people began living beyond retirement age, it opened up a whole new way of approaching 'the rest of their lives.'

Unfortunately, too few people look forward to the freedom of this period and see it primarily as a time of loss—when they're no longer needed or wanted. Much of this is due to the connotations of 'retirement' as somehow ceasing to be a vital part of society as a whole.

This negative mindset about retirement is reflected in the way it's defined in the dictionary:

—to dispose of something no longer useful or needed
—to stop performing one's work
—to go into privacy; as, to retire to his home; to retire from the world or from notice
—to withdraw, as from worldly matters or the company of others

This theme was continued in a recent television commercial, depicting retirement as a time to withdraw, to go away, to disappear.

However, in accordance with the ideas in the book, "My Time," I encourage everyone to look forward to that period as a

## MUSINGS ON LIFE

time for seeking purpose, finding meaning, giving back, expanding the mind and leaving a legacy.

## Chapter 3: On Being a Woman

Women of Courage
Respecting Women's Choices
'Working' Mothers
Balancing Home and Work
Dancing as Fast as I Can
Spending Time Alone
It's Not Easy Being a Woman

*On Being a Woman*

**Women of Courage**  January 2008

When we think of courage, the image that first comes to mind is likely to be that of a soldier or some other hero figure, usually male. But courage comes in many forms—and in both genders. Today I want to focus on *women* of courage.

This focus is prompted at this time by recent events that put a spotlight on a true woman of courage, Benazir Bhutto. She's the former twice prime minister of Pakistan who was assassinated only a couple of months after returning to Pakistan from a self-imposed exile.

Everyone, including Benazir Bhutto, recognized that she was a target and that her return was at great personal risk. However, she demonstrated the courage of her convictions by returning anyway—because she felt it was her duty to try to be elected Prime Minister again in the scheduled general election.

There had been an assassination attempt upon her arrival in the country in October, and while others in her entourage were killed, she escaped that attempt. There were constant threats on her life, but she didn't let that stand in the way of getting out among the people to rally them to support her cause and her party. It was at just such a rally where an assassination attempt succeeded.

Her awareness of the risk was underscored in a recent interview with Ann Curry of NBC News in which she talked calmly about the choice she was making to continue her quest, despite the risks to her life. In fact, the words and the manner in which she spoke were reminiscent of Martin Luther King, Jr.'s speech the night before he was assassinated.

While these larger-than-life figures stand out as special in the courage they display, there are many women who demonstrate extraordinary courage in their daily lives. In fact, I can point to one in my own family who was amazing in the strength and courage she displayed in simply 'doing what had to be done.'

My grandmother had nine children—one of which she delivered herself while her husband had gone to get the doctor. Her husband was very little help in providing financially for the family, so it was left to her to be the primary provider as well. She worked at many jobs, one of which involved sewing dresses for other people—often completing two or three dresses in a day!

But it was her fierce determination that was most amazing. For instance, when my father was a teenager, he badly burned one arm. The doctor said since the skin could never grow back, he had to amputate the arm. But my grandmother refused, saying she would hold his arm up off the bed as long as it took for the skin to grow back. Nobody knows how she did it, but she sat by his bed round-the-clock for as long as it took to begin the healing process—and saved his arm.

Then in her later years (in her 80s and 90s), she was completely blind and lived with one of her daughters—but managed to fend for herself all day every day while her daughter was at work.

Other women in my family have also demonstrated courage in difficult times. And my awareness of the strong stock of women who came before me gives me a great deal of inspiration to be strong in facing anything life might bring my way.

I'm sure everyone can think of women friends and family members who've shown extraordinary courage. So I hope you'll pause to reflect on the examples of courage you know about personally—in hopes that you'll be inspired to be more courageous in your own life.

On Being a Woman

\* \* \* \* \* \* \* \* \*

**Respecting Women's Choices         April 2007**

This past week I read an article in my local paper about 'How U.S. society fails mothers.' Basically, it was covering the work of Ann Crittenden (a Pulitzer Prize nominee and former reporter for the New York Times) who has written a number of books about the dilemma of being a 'mother' in today's world. Some of her books include: "The Price of Motherhood: Why The Most Important Job in the World is Still the Least Valued" and "If you've Raised Kids, You can Manage Anything: Leadership Begins at Home."

This article set me thinking about my own life experience as a woman and mother, as well as that of my daughter—and also wondering what it will be like for my granddaughters when they grow up. It seems to me that many things about 'women's choices' have changed substantially—while others have not.

For instance, women today generally *choose* whether or not to have children. This was not something I saw as a choice when I married at age 19. I simply *assumed* I'd have children; it was only a matter of when and how many. Of course, I can't imagine not having my two terrific grown kids, but the point is still well-taken that when I was a young married woman this was not a conscious choice.

However, even now that women make more conscious choices about such significant life decisions, our choices often divide us into two opposing groups—each somewhat suspicious of the other. For instance, when it comes to motherhood, in an effort to defend our own choice we often become critical of those who choose differently.

While this criticism may seem unreasonable and petty, it's often prompted by our need to validate the correctness of our own decision. We may try to guarantee our satisfaction with the decision by convincing ourselves that it was the *right* one—and that those who didn't choose as we did are *wrong*. To further complicate this issue, there are many women who didn't actually 'choose' their situations. There are mothers who didn't intend to get pregnant, and there are women who desperately want to have a child, but can't get pregnant or can't carry a child to term.

But the bottom line is that no decision is more personal or individual than whether or not to become a mother. And if we're satisfied with our own choice, we need not attack those who choose differently. In fact, we need to be more than just tolerant of women who make a decision different from our own. We need to respect each other for the difficult choices we have to make—and support each other in seeking the most satisfying ways of living with our choices.

Also, it's important to recognize that as women we play a lot of different roles at different stages of our lives. As I look back on my own life, I realize that although I'm still very much a 'mother,' this is not my primary role in life as it was during the 20 years I spent caring for children living at home. At age 71, it's easy for me to see the shortsightedness of allowing our different life choices to stand in the way of recognizing the common dilemmas we all face as women.

\* \* \* \* \* \* \* \* \*

## 'Working' Mothers                    July 2007

*All* mothers 'work'—so it's important to clarify that this discussion is not about whether or not to 'work,' but whether or not to work 'outside the home.'

Unfortunately, this is another significant choice that often divides women between those who choose to be full-time homemakers and those who work outside the home. While single mothers may not have a choice, many women criticize those who make a choice different from their own. But the same general observations apply with this situation as with whether or not to be a mother: *every choice involves trade-offs and we need to respect each woman's decision based on her assessment of her own situation.*

Of course, just as some women don't actually choose whether or not to become a mother (due to circumstances beyond their control), circumstances may also dictate whether or not a mother works outside the home—with finances often playing a central role.

I've had a long-time interest in this issue, at one point even having a website focusing on work/family dilemmas. Also, of course, I've had personal experience in this juggling act myself. And my experience is fairly common in that most women do *both* (stay at home full-time *and* work outside the home) at different points in their lives.

I worked the first seven years of marriage to help put my husband through graduate school. Our first child was born one week after he completed his Ph.D., and I was thrilled to become a stay-at-home mother. With a second child being born a couple of years later (and James's income making it possible), I continued to be a stay-at-home mother.

Then about the same time our youngest began first grade, James left his job as a professor and became an independent consultant. Without money to hire enough people in his work, I stepped in and worked with him five days a week, leaving early each afternoon to be home when the kids got out of school. In later years, we had our office at home, so I continued to be able to work and still be a stay-at-home mother. I was very fortunate and recognize that this was a rare opportunity not afforded to most women.

An additional benefit of our home office was that James got to be a stay-at-home dad as well—which is another important issue that needs a great deal more attention. But the focus for now is still on the dilemma facing mothers who work outside the home.

This issue continues to be the source of much discussion and investigation. In fact, a new study just released from the Pew Research Center pointed out that *most* women would prefer to be able to have a part-time job. Specifically, the report says, *"60 percent of the working moms said they would rather spend more time with family by working part-time."*

To quote more of the comments related to the study:

*"While other women may dream of that kind of schedule, they may not have a choice or an option to cut their work hours. Financial realities and today's competitive workplace can preclude some from a part-time schedule, leaving women to struggle to find the right balance between home and work. I think everybody steps back sometimes and says, 'Did I make the right choice?' The second-guessing may always be there—but so is the joy of being a mother."*

As stated by Leslie Bennetts, author of "The Feminine Mistake," *"These choices are so hard for women, and women are made to feel guilty, no matter what they do."*

So rather than criticizing other women for their choices, we need to have a great deal of compassion for the struggle we all make as 'working women'—whether or not it involves working 'outside the home.' We all know the most important work we'll ever do (with the longest-lasting relevance and importance for the future) is our work as mothers. In the final analysis, what binds us together as mothers is far greater than any of our different choices.

\* \* \* \* \* \* \* \* \*

**Balancing Home and Work**                           **April 2007**

During the 70s and early 80s, I worked as a corporate consultant on male-female issues—and one of those 'issues' involved balancing work life with home life. This is a difficult dilemma, requiring making many choices and trade-offs in order to lead a more fulfilling, less harried life.

Trying to live a 'balanced life' does not mean reaching some kind of static point. For instance, an airplane that's on course is almost never *exactly* on course. The pilot makes thousands of minute adjustments. Balance is about not getting so far in one extreme that you have to go to the other extreme to find some sort of equanimity.

When people feel stressed by the demands of their lives, they tend to resort to overeating, overdrinking, getting too little (or too much) sleep, and other self-defeating tactics. Unfortunately, all of those efforts to escape the situation wind up working against getting control of your life.

One of the reasons it's so difficult to make choices aimed at achieving balance is that there are always trade-offs to whatever choice you make. And you do always make a choice (even when it doesn't feel that way) because *not* making a choice is still 'choosing' by default.

There are certain actions that we understandably don't see as being a choice—like abandoning our responsibilities to our family. But some people with financial and family responsibilities *do* step off the track. They may walk away from their families, just disappearing and leaving the family to pick up the pieces. So it's not that you don't have a choice. It's that you're not willing to accept the trade-offs involved in making certain choices. So recognizing that you do have a choice (and that you *are* making choices) can help avoid feeling helpless and out of control.

While every choice is based on our individual values, we don't necessarily act in accordance with our *stated* values. Our real values are reflected in the way we use our time. For instance, if you hear someone say, "I value my family most of all," but that person works 60+ hours each week, then that's not really their value system. It just indicates a value to which they *aspire*, not a value they're actually living.

Unfortunately, many people justify the time they put into their work, saying the extreme amounts of time and effort are essential to building and maintaining a career. But that way of thinking illustrates how we've come to view what's 'important' in life. For instance, who says being a top-notch attorney is more important than being a stay-at-home mom? We have to break through those assumptions and overcome the pressures to do what society rewards. Aspiring to gain society's recognition of certain achievements often comes at a very high price. Those who excel in a significant way in one particular area invariably make enormous trade-offs, cutting off satisfaction in many other areas of life.

## On Being a Woman

Since men particularly are rewarded for their career achievements, a man's identity has often been defined by how successful he is in his job. Therefore, many men are reluctant to use flex time or other time off that may be offered by their companies. For instance, if a man takes advantage of the Family and Medical Leave Act, he's judged more harshly than a woman who's trying to have that kind of balance. And everybody loses. Until men are more equally responsible at home, women cannot be equally successful at work. In fact, most working women who are also mothers are absolutely exhausted most of the time.

Men and women have to ask both their employer and their family for what they need. First, get your values and priorities straight. Second, share with others what you need and want—because people can sabotage your efforts without even knowing it. And third, go about pursuing what you want and need; don't expect someone to give it to you. (This is a special challenge for women, leading to a great deal of dissatisfaction.) It's critical to take responsibility for making choices that are based on your own priorities in life.

One of the reasons to get comfortable with making your own choices and deciding on your own trade-offs (rather than going along with what others may choose for you) is that a lack of control makes people unhappy and depressed. If you think you don't have a choice, then write down what you *wish* you could do. Then write down what you actually do. Compare the two lists—not focusing on which list is longest, but on which has the most significant items. This can enable you to more clearly establish your priorities and serve as a guide in making decisions based on your own personal values.

We live in such a fast-paced society, such a 'now' culture, that we tend to focus on the moment. But when you get to be my age, you realize there are many phases of life. So while you may not be able to have everything you want 'all at the same time,' you can make different choices for different periods. For instance, if you give up something during one period of your life, you may be able to come back to it later.

So when trying to balance home and work, it can be very helpful to take this long view and large sweep of life. This perspective can allow you to make decisions with the bigger picture in mind rather than just reacting to life's immediate pressures.

\* \* \* \* \* \* \* \* \*

**Dancing as Fast as I Can**  **March 2008**

The title of this column is the same as the title of a book by Barbara Gordon that was published many years ago. The book told the true story of the author's devastating reaction to going 'cold turkey' after being addicted to prescription drugs. But through the years it's come to represent the way many women feel about their lives in general—constantly rushing and 'dancing as fast as they can' just to keep up.

I've been feeling that way lately—even more than usual. For better or worse, I tend to be very conscientious about keeping up to date on all my responsibilities. Of course, realistically that's an impossible standard to apply to your daily life. While I realize my In-box will never be empty, I still tend to put enormous pressure on myself to complete everything as quickly as possible.

I'm very much like most women in that I wind up feeling that I'm running around in circles, trying to wear a lot of different hats. (All you women reading this know exactly what

## On Being a Woman

I mean.) We play so many different roles—with many of them feeling quite incongruous—that we almost feel like we have split personalities. That's what's been happening to me recently as I've been caught up in focusing on quite different areas of my life.

For instance, just as I was writing the above, I responded to an urgent request from a major news magazine for an interview—and rushed through it to dash out the door to attend a sports event to watch one of my grandchildren.

There's an old saying that reflects the way a lot of women feel today, *"Man may work from sun to sun, but a woman's work is never done."*

While there have been dramatic changes through the years in the way *both* men and women work outside the home and within the home, most women still recognize that, in general, women tend to do much more.

But this is *not* about saying what men should or shouldn't do. I only want to focus on the fact that we women need to give ourselves a break from the many demands we make on ourselves—not only to *do* a lot of things, but to do them all extremely well. We can't seem to accept that 'good enough' is often actually good enough!

So I invite all women to join me in trying to be less demanding of ourselves by recognizing that if we don't pause to fill ourselves up occasionally, we may run out of steam and not be able to continue to respond to others.

Frankly, others don't really appreciate (or even want) us being so rushed and frazzled. Most of our friends and family would rather have us be more relaxed and available instead of trying to figure out how we can dance even faster.

\* \* \* \* \* \* \* \* \*

## Spending Time Alone    December 2006

I'm alone this week—and loving it. (James has gone to Mississippi to be with his Mother who's celebrating her 99th Birthday!) It's clear to me that I don't want to be alone *all* the time, but it's lovely to have these little periods of alone-time, all the while knowing that your loved one will return.

I realize that not everyone values time alone. They equate being alone with being lonely. I've never felt lonely when I've been alone. Frankly, the most peaceful times of my life (when I've done the deepest thinking and experienced just 'being there') have occurred during those periods when I've been by myself.

So I'm using this opportunity to deliberately seek ways to be calmer and slow down a bit. I tend to always be rushing around—which can be very tiring, not only for me but also for those around me.

I know that part of my intensity is because I keep myself on such a tightly-defined schedule. I tend to plan each day's activities very carefully, constantly checking the time—this despite the fact that I don't have to answer to anyone about my use of time. So I'm using this period alone to try to change that.

The first thing I did was to remove my watch and cover the faces of all the clocks in the house, including the computer clock. I even covered the clock in the car. (I realized how time-obsessed I was when I found that this involved twelve different timepieces!)

The first couple of days I felt strangely anxious and uncertain, still contemplating what time it might be—and still making plans for what to do when. It's a very different experience, trying to base my actions on being in touch with what feels right rather than on what the clock says. For

## On Being a Woman

instance, I don't know what time I get up in the morning, don't know what time I go to bed at night, and don't know what time I eat my meals.

Anyway, I'm finally beginning to settle into this new situation where I'm acting in a more conscious manner. And sure enough, I'm finding that it's allowing me to slow down a bit and feel a little calmer. The surprising (and very satisfying) bonus is that this way of operating is leading me to be far more productive than usual.

Of course, I realize that the degree to which this can be pursued depends on other life situations. But I recommend more alone-time for anyone who feels overwhelmed with the rush of daily life.

I used to think there was something weird about my desire to carve out times when I could be alone. But then I began to notice that many women have expressed the same sentiments. So I'd like to share some of the writings of two women with whom I identify.

The first is May Sarton. She lived alone for many years and wrote about it in several of her books, most notably her "Journal of a Solitude."

*"For a long time now, every meeting with another human being has been a collision. I feel too much, sense too much, am exhausted by the reverberations after even the simplest conversation. I find that when I have an appointment, even an afternoon one, it changes the whole quality of time. I feel overcharged. There is no space for what wells up from the subconscious; those dreams and images live in deep still water and simply submerge when the day gets scattered. There are times lately when I dream only of disappearing, taking another name, settling in to some place where no one would recognize me or care."*

Barbara Lazear Ascher also wrote movingly about the way many women (busy wives and mothers) think about solitude. Here's a passage from her book, "Playing After Dark."

*"I have a friend, happily married, who says that she can't imagine leaving her husband for another man. What she can imagine is leaving him for solitude. It's harder to win than a lover, but it may better nourish the soul. If my friend left, her husband might find it hard to believe that it was a quest for solitude rather than sexual adventure that called her away.*

*"If a woman had the choice of a week without solitude or a week without lusty encounter, chances are she would elect the latter. Given the choice. There is a tree in our park favored by birds...it sways with the ruckus of sparrows and finches. This tree reminds me of a woman's life.*

*"We welcome the hubbub and resonance of other lives, unfold our limbs to support and hold them. The air around us fills with chattering distraction. We encourage intimacies, bask in companionship, tales, details, news. We were the first to tell our children stories and then listen when they returned the favor. We taught them the pleasure of repartee and charmed them with our company. They were trained to seek us out, to gather round our table, settle into our laps.*

*"There's a lot to be said for being needed. Being the caretaker of others' souls gives one a sense of purpose and worth. A tree is less a tree in the absence of birds. And yet, as the business of others' lives gathers round, settles into our branches and begins to hum, we long, at times, for silence... We long to be separated by a sea or plains, mountains or river, to put the distance of the road between*

*ourselves and those whose melodies we can't resist, whose choruses we join, drowning out ourselves in the uproar.*

*"It is a need to find and sing our own song, to stretch our limbs and shake them in a dance so wild that nothing can roost there, that stirs the yearnings for solitary voyage... It is to discover that we are capable of solitary joy and having experienced it, know that we have touched the core of self."*

\* \* \* \* \* \* \* \* \*

**It's Not Easy Being a Woman**           **February 2007**

The many roles women play cause us to feel constantly rushed, trying to keep up with what's going on in our lives. For me personally, it's always been much easier whenever I was in the (rare) position of focusing on only *one* responsibility at a time—like the many instances when I sat with my mother in the hospital and really *couldn't* do anything else.

But most days I feel very fragmented as I jump from one area to another. At one moment I'm a doting mother and grandmother and the next I'm a serious 'professional.' For instance, when I go from babysitting my grandchildren to immediately doing a telephone consultation, it feels a little schizophrenic.

While those are just the most obvious switches in my persona, like most women, there are many others. I'm also strongly committed to staying informed about current news and important developments around the world, keeping up with entertainment trivia, exercising to stay fit and healthy, as well as being a wife, mother and grandmother.

Actually, I'm not too concerned about all of this—because I think it's normal for women to feel so fragmented. Sometimes I even find humor in reflecting on the old Peggy Lee song, "Cause I'm a Woman." Below is just one of the verses of this song:

> *"I can rub and scrub till this old house*
> *Is shinin' like a dime*
> *Feed the baby, grease the car and*
> *Powder my face at the same time.*
> *Get all dressed up, go out and swing*
> *Till four a.m. and then*
> *Lay down at five, jump up at six*
> *And start all over again.*
> *'Cause I'm a woman*
> *W O M A N*
> *I'll say it again*
> *'Cause I'm a woman*
> *W O M A N*
> *And that's all."*

I'm not complaining about being a woman. I feel about being a woman a little like Kermit the Frog feels about being green. Here's the final line from his song "It's Not that Easy Being Green."

> *"I am green and it'll do fine, it's beautiful*
> *And I think it's what I want to be."*

# Chapter 4: Love/Relationships

Marrying Young
Valentine's Day Thoughts
The Power of a Kiss
Sleep (the Cuddle Factor)
Love, Sweet Love
Lessons in Love
Friends
Love and Devotion

*Love/Relationships*

## Marrying Young                                May 2007

Today is our 52nd Wedding Anniversary, and I'm reflecting on the fact that we married so young! We were both only 19 years old when we got married. (Actually, our *first* marriage was even young than that—when we were about 6 years old. Our neighborhood of kids decided to have a 'Tom Thumb Wedding,' and since we were little sweethearts, we were the bride and groom.)

In hindsight, it's clear that we were far too young to marry. We weren't fully-formed individuals with a sense of our own separate identity. And such an early marriage was particularly problematic for me as a woman of the 50s in that I went straight from my father's house to my husband's—which lead me to identify with my role (first as 'daughter,' then as 'wife') without ever establishing my own identity as an independent person.

However, with all the drawbacks to marrying so young, it can *also* create a special bond and connection that may be more difficult to establish when you meet your future spouse as an adult. For instance, when the inevitable stresses of life threaten a marriage, the additional connection by virtue of forging a strong identity as a couple rather than as an individual does make it easier for your spouse to also be your best friend.

So the strong love that prompted us to marry at a young age has helped sustain us throughout our married life. We not only have the bond created by virtue of being a couple and having children together, but we have the additional bond of having known each other *all* our lives. It's the kind of lifelong closeness that normally only develops between blood relatives.

Most people recognize that the feelings they had (and still fondly recall) for their 'first love' is a powerful force, and many people try to reconnect with the person who holds this special place in their lives. In fact, a lot of people are finding their first love through the Internet and reconnecting after many years. This sometimes turns out wonderfully when both are single and available, leading to successful marriages. On the other hand, when one or both are married, the power of this reconnection can lead to distress and/or divorce.

At this point in my life, I'm thankful to have married young and to have stayed married all these years, but I do *not* recommend it. We were one of the lucky couples for whom the strength of our early bond was more positive and powerful than the drawbacks to marrying so young. So we strongly encouraged our own daughter to wait, and she was 24 at the time of her marriage 20 years ago.

I do see a trend from generation to generation regarding the common age for getting married. For instance, my mother married at 15, I married at 19 and my daughter married at 24. And since life expectancy continues to increase, it should still be possible to have a 50+ year marriage without marrying young.

\* \* \* \* \* \* \* \* \*

**Valentine's Day Thoughts**  February 2007

One of the key events in the month of February is Valentine's Day—which holds different meanings for different people. Little children enjoy exchanging cards with their friends, and married people (and others in committed relationships) may pause to acknowledge their love bond.

But the primary push behind Valentine's Day is the appeal to those newly 'in love'—usually those who are still in the

*Love/Relationships*

initial two-year period of their relationship and are caught up in the excitement of the newness of the connection.

This two-year time period is not arbitrary; it conforms to the scientifically-based information about romantic love that's been growing in recent years. For the most comprehensive understanding of this concept, I highly recommend a book by Helen Fisher, "Why we Love: The Nature and Chemistry of Romantic Love."

Simply put, there are different brain chemicals that determine the different stages of love. The chemicals that determine romantic passion are different from those that gradually transform passion into feelings of deep attachment. The chemicals of romantic love are stimulated by the excitement of the newness and novelty. But this doesn't last beyond about two years. Then it ends, allowing the possibility of being transformed into the kind of love that creates a more lasting bond.

\* \* \* \* \* \* \* \* \*

**The Power of a Kiss** February 2007

While Valentine's Day may be an important part of the courting ritual, for long-term relationships it seldom has the same degree of importance.

There are many reasons why we tend to lose the excitement and passion of the early days of the relationship—and one small part of that may be that we have failed to honor the power of a kiss.

'A Kiss is Just a Kiss' is the subtitle of an old song recorded by Louis Armstrong titled "As Time Goes By."

However, that sentiment is absolutely wrong—particularly when it comes to its impact on women.

While men may be goal-oriented when it comes to passion, women are much more whole-body-oriented. So 'the kiss' takes on a special significance for women. In fact, a soft, slow kiss, especially with a full-body hug, may be the most important key to unlocking a woman's passion.

For many women, their early years where kissing was the 'main event' linger as a wonderful memory of the desire resulting from those kisses. Then after many years into a relationship or a long-term marriage, the kisses may become more perfunctory—and therefore fail to provide the basis for passion and desire. (It's not surprising that prostitutes have a general rule against kissing—since they don't want to develop any real feelings for their partners.)

So even though our lives may be rushed and filled with responsibilities that distract us and tire us out, we can re-energize our feelings of passion by remembering to honor the power of a kiss. In fact, it's smart to engage in at least one real kiss (not a quick peck) every day, making it a daily habit.

This certainly doesn't indicate sexual activity on a daily basis, but it keeps the pilot light burning for those times when sex does get on the agenda. And in the meantime, you're likely to feel closer to your partner and better able to deal with other issues as they arise.

The bottom line is to recognize the importance of long-lasing love every day of the year—not just on Valentine's Day. In fact, I personally value expressions of love at unexpected times throughout the year far more than the ritualized expressions so common on Valentine's Day. And a real, genuine, lingering kiss is just the kind of expression of love that can really make a difference.

*Love/Relationships*

\* \* \* \* \* \* \* \* \*

**Sleep (the Cuddle Factor)**  February 2007

Sleep plays a very important role in allowing us to face each new day with the energy needed to go about our daily activities. Maybe one of the reasons little children have so much energy is that they're able to fall into a deep sleep and sleep straight through the night (after the first few months, of course). In fact, when my grandchildren come over to spend the night, I'm fascinated by the way they can sleep so soundly throughout the night.

Once we become adults, we frequently go to bed with lots of thoughts racing around in our heads of what we need to do the next day—or failed to do the day before. All this thinking can make it hard to settle down and get to sleep in the first place, or to stay asleep once we doze off.

Frequently, the problems with sleep simply increase as we get older. For several years, I've had trouble sleeping. While I can usually go to sleep OK, I awaken many times throughout the night—and often have great difficulty getting back to sleep. I've even gotten into the bad habit of getting up for an hour or so in the middle of the night, hoping to get sleepy again. I do have a rule of only resorting to getting up if I've been lying awake in bed for at least an hour.

I've tried some of the common techniques for getting to sleep (like visualization, having a cup of hot tea, listening to soothing music, and avoiding TV or other stimulating activities just prior to retiring)—but none of them work in a reliable way. I blame part of this on the fact that I'm a pretty intense person most of the time and generally have a difficult time just relaxing.

However, I've found that a much less well-known (but very effective) way of inducing sleep is simply cuddling. James and I have always had a habit of spending a few minutes when we first awaken in the morning just cuddling, usually in the spoon position. But lately we've begun deliberately using it to go to sleep in the middle of the night when one of us wakes up and can't get back to sleep. It works every time, and we can continue it for hours—even turning back and forth in sync throughout the night without getting fully awake.

Of course, in addition to being an effective factor in conquering sleeplessness, it's also a wonderful way to reinforce the closeness of the relationship. So whether or not you have trouble sleeping, I think you'll find great benefit from including the 'cuddle factor' in your own loving relationship.

Since skin-on-skin contact is a contributing factor in the calming, sleep-inducing power of cuddling, I recommend that you sleep without clothing—or at least with as minimal amount as your lifestyle allows.

Our own experience throughout our 51 years of marriage has been to sleep in the nude, and I credit it with contributing to the physical connection we've been able to sustain through all the ups and downs of our marriage.

\* \* \* \* \* \* \* \* \*

**Love, Sweet Love**  **September 2007**

Last night my husband and I watched a movie called "Away from Her" that dealt with the impact of Alzheimer's on a long-term marriage. The most striking and most touching aspect of the movie (starring Julie Christie as an aging wife with Alzheimer's) was the pure *sweetness* of the love demonstrated

*Love/Relationships*

by her husband in the way he eventually dealt with the situation, sacrificing his own personal needs in order to do what his wife needed. This was particularly poignant in view of an earlier period of their marriage where he'd been quite selfish.

This movie provides a real lesson in what 'sweet love' is all about. I'm sure that my using the word *sweet* to try to describe this particular demonstration of love is due to the songs that tend to jump to mind on most any topic—in this case Burt Bacharach's "What the World Needs Now Is Love, Sweet Love."

Another song that relates to the kind of gentle caring associated with such a sweet love is one by the Beatles, "Will you still need me, Will you still feed me, When I'm sixty-four?"

None of us wants to think we'll ever face a situation that calls for such a deep degree of caring and unselfish giving of ourselves. Of course, we also don't want to think of being the one who needs this kind of caring. But the reality is that Alzheimer's and other debilitating illnesses are realistic possibilities for the future.

When we're younger, we tend to think of love in terms of 'romantic love' with all its excitement, largely focused on what our love relationship does for *us*. But when faced with challenges later in life, the romantic love won't be of much benefit—because the kind of love needed at that stage is one largely focused on what our love relationship allows us to do for our loved one.

While it's beautiful to see an older couple exhibiting such deep caring for each other, unfortunately, we also see older couples who not only fail to be kind to each other, but have become quite bitter, snapping at each other over all kinds of petty issues.

Since we tend to reap what we sow, I hope all couples (even if still in the earlier stages of your love relationship) will recognize that the nature of the love you're building during the good times sets the stage for the time when your love may be tested by adversity such as Alzheimer's.

\* \* \* \* \* \* \* \* \*

**Lessons in Love** November 2007

Many of us find it easy to say "I love you." But saying these words is not nearly as important as showing our love through actions. Since 'actions speak louder than words,' the evidence of our love is not in what we say, but in what we do—especially when times are difficult.

A wonderful 'lesson in love' is to be found in the reaction by Retired Justice Sandra Day O'Connor to the actions of her husband of 55 years who is in a facility for people with Alzheimer's. He's begun a romance with a woman at the facility, and his son describes him as behaving like 'a teenager in love.'

Justice O'Connor recognizes that Alzheimer's patients who forget their spouses often fall in love with someone else. So instead of being upset by this development, her son reports that she is *"thrilled that Dad was relaxed and happy and comfortable living here and wasn't complaining. For Mom to visit when he's happy ... visiting with his girlfriend, sitting on the porch swing holding hands, was a relief after a painful period."*

*Love/Relationships*

She recognizes that this has nothing to do with her or in any way diminishes the love they shared for so many years. To her enormous credit she has not taken his actions personally—a beautiful example of the second agreement in Don Miguel Ruiz's book, "The Four Agreements:" 'Don't take anything personally'

All too often, our love relationships are more about what *we* want or need in the relationship rather than what is best for our spouse. But genuine love wants only the best for the beloved, even when it may not be what we want or need personally for ourselves.

It should be noted that this is not the first time Justice O'Connor has demonstrated this kind of selfless love for her husband. Her retirement from the Supreme Court in 2006 was prompted only by her desire to care for him as his Alzheimer's progressed.

While this kind of selfless love is easy to accept in theory, putting it into practice is a rare and beautiful lesson in love. Justice O'Connor's example of her deep and abiding love for her husband can serve as an inspiration for all of us as we seek to more genuinely express our love.

\* \* \* \* \* \* \* \* \*

**Friends** October 2007

When we speak of relationships, we usually think of *love* relationships. While I highly value my lifelong love relationship with my husband, other relationships in our lives also play an important role. For instance, as a mother, my relationship with my adult children is still of critical importance to me. In fact, I spend a good bit of time with them, as well as devoting time and energy in being supportive of them.

But when it comes to friends, I have very few—only those with whom I can share *anything* and who have the same 'take' on life when it comes to the 'big issues.' While I interact with a lot of people through my work, I only have a handful of 'counting friends'—those I can literally count on one hand. In fact, I believe that if a person has up to five real counting friends, they're very fortunate.

There was a time earlier in my life when I was involved with a lot of other people, particularly when my kids were small. In fact, our house was like Grand Central Station, and I valued that for their sake. Our house was also the place where everyone gathered for social activities and neighborhood get-togethers. But I was seldom really close to anyone during that period, and, in fact, rather than enjoying all the socialization, it was quite a strain.

Part of the reason for the stress of these social interactions was that I felt I was not being authentic. I was behaving as people are expected to behave in social settings, keeping it light and pleasant and avoiding anything too deep or meaningful. While I've always been quite socially skilled (and, in fact, people would assume I was an extrovert), it was not reflective of my real feelings

So for many years now I've resisted making new friends, preferring to invest myself in my long-time friends who have known me well over many years. Since we've all moved a lot through the years, this means I seldom see my friends face to face. But our relationships are deep and meaningful, and completely satisfy my desire for this kind of connection. Part of the reason this situation suits me so well is that I have a strong need for a lot of alone-time.

*Love/Relationships*

In fact, my need for time alone is so great that if I spend a full day interacting with others, I need several hours alone to 'decompress' before I can go to bed at night. I think the reason I need time to calm down before retiring is due to the intensity with which I engage others. Ironically, I've found that I invest the same amount of focus and energy in interacting with one person as in speaking to a thousand. It's all the same when it comes to the impact on me and my need to settle down after the encounter.

All this may sound strange to people on the other end of the spectrum who love having people around them all the time. Some people simply hate being alone for any extended period, and others equate being alone with being lonely. But for me, the answer to the question in the old Patsy Cline song, "Have you ever been lonely?"—is no. I'm quite at peace when I'm alone.

I do recognize that moderation is the key for any healthy way of being in the world. Too much or too little time alone (or with others) may not serve us well as humans. It's wise to be deliberate in assessing your own personal preferences and taking the steps that are needed to get more of whatever is important to you.

If your life is absorbed in always being around others, you might consider whether you could benefit from some time alone. And if you're alone (and lonely), you might consider ways to develop more relationships to fill this void in your life. Too often we go along with our current situation regarding our relationships without consciously choosing and actively seeking whatever we personally need in this area.

So I hope you'll reflect on your own life and the way you spend your time (alone and with others) and consider whether you want to make any changes. If so, I hope you take steps to seek whatever balance suits you best.

* * * * * * * * *

**Love and Devotion**                                           **March 2008**

When we think of love, we think of the kind of romantic love contained in Elizabeth Barrett Browning's "How do I love thee? Let me count the ways." But words are not nearly as powerful in demonstrating the depth of love as are actions. And when it comes to actions, there's no greater love than that of 'man's best friend,' the faithful dog. (If you're not a 'dog person,' you may not fully appreciate the sentiments that follow—but please bear with me.)

My appreciation for the special love between humans and their dogs began when I was a child, only seven years old. I had a little dog that I loved—and he loved me back. But when he began acting strangely, my parents penned him up in the back yard and told me not to go near him. Nevertheless, one day when he looked very lonely and forlorn, I *did* go to him. As I kneeled down to pet him, he suddenly bit me on the cheek.

It turns out he had been bitten by a rabid wild animal—and had developed rabies himself. This meant that every day for three weeks I had to take anti-rabies shots, which were given in my back with a very long needle. While I didn't cry about the shots, I did cry when they had to put my beloved dog to sleep. You see, even as a child, I *knew* my dog loved me with all his heart and would never have hurt me on purpose.

This experience might have killed my love of dogs, but it would have been a great loss—because through the years I've

*Love/Relationships*

had several other dogs, each quite special in their love and devotion.

For instance, supposedly dogs don't have an awareness of the passage of time. But I had an experience with a dog that belies that belief. After I married, our first dog was particularly devoted to us, and it came as a great disappointment to have to part with him for one summer while we worked at a facility that included room and board—but did not allow dogs. So we shipped our 'George' to my parents for the summer.

George's pain at being away from us was so great that he hardly ate, and my folks were concerned that he was going to grieve himself to death. (They kept this from me, or I might have given up the summer job.) Anyway, sure enough, his reaction when we returned to pick him up was one of the most overwhelming responses I've ever seen—from either human or animal. He was a large German Shepherd, and he stood up on his hind paws, put his front paws up on my shoulders, licked my face—and 'wailed' (the kind of wailing you hear from humans in war-torn countries when there's a massacre of their loved ones). His demonstration of love was absolutely overwhelming.

Much later, we had another dog with a very mellow personality. In fact, we named him Captain Easy because he was so easygoing. We kidded that he must be some kind of mystic—like a yogi. And he was tremendously independent. Once when we went out of town for a couple of weeks on a family vacation, we had a house-sitter come stay in our home, primarily to avoid having to board Captain Easy.

Well, a few days after we left town, Captain Easy disappeared. The young woman assigned to take care of him was distraught and did everything possible to find him and entice him back home—all to no avail. But within an hour of our return, Captain Easy turned up on the porch—ten days after he had disappeared. We never knew how he managed during the time he was gone. But it seems clear that he only wanted to be there when *we* were there. Clearly, he loved us and was completely devoted to being with us—and only us.

While I value my personal experiences with my dogs, I'm overwhelmed by a couple of stories I recently read—where dogs showed such enormous devotion as to be almost unbelievable, but true nonetheless.

One of the most amazing examples of devotion was that of a dog in Japan, an unusual breed called Akita. This dog lived with his owner, a noted professor there. When the professor died, his dog continued to meet his master's four o'clock commuter train at the station every day—for the next nine years!

Another touching story about the strong bond between man and dog comes from Iraq where an American soldier tended to the war-wounds of a dog there, and the dog became completely devoted to him. In fact, his devotion was so great that when the soldier was moved to an area of Iraq 65 miles away, the dog found his way to him. (We hear humans say they 'will follow their loved one to the ends of the earth,' but this dog actually did!)

And I just learned of a book that makes a very strong point about the power of a dog's devotion. It's called "Puppy Chow is Better than Prozac: The True Story of a Man and the Dog Who Saved His Life." Here's part of the description: *"Meet Ozzy. For the suicidally depressed author, this furry antidepressant came with only one side effect—unconditional, slobbery love."*

*Love/Relationships*

In reflecting on these stories, I think you'll agree that we humans can learn something from our four-footed friends about unconditional love and devotion.

## Chapter 5: Family

Family Patterns
Family Gatherings
Family Keepsakes
Mother's Day
Special Memories
Who You Gonna Call?
Running with the Boys
The Soccer Generation
Children without Families
Happy 100th Birthday!

*Family*

**Family Patterns**                                                **August 2006**

The nature of modern life significantly alters the living patterns of most families in the U.S. And while some cultures of the world still maintain a strong continuation of the same patterns within families, the rapidly-changing lifestyles and technologies are having an impact almost everywhere.

For instance, the Internet allows us to have a much greater awareness of and involvement with worldwide issues. Growing up in a small town in Mississippi (population 5,000) was a very different kind of experience. For instance, I knew everyone in town and everyone knew me.

My children grew up in Hilton Head Island, SC, where they knew most of the people with whom they came in contact during the winter. But since it was a resort area, the summer population was quite large and significantly changed the experience for those of us who were full-time residents.

Now my grandchildren live in several worlds. One is their immediate tight-knit neighborhood where (like in my own childhood) everyone knows everyone else. Another is the larger city of which their neighborhood is a part and where they move among a wider circle of people. And finally, they also live in the much broader plugged-in culture through TV, cell phones, the Internet, etc.

In fact, it's hard for them to believe—or even to completely comprehend—that there was no TV when I was growing up. At first, they thought I must mean there were no movies on DVD or ability to *record* TV shows. But they gradually came to realize that I never saw a TV show while I was growing up in the 40s and early 50s; it wasn't until after I married in 1955 that we got our first used television set.

One thing that has helped to bridge these very different childhood experiences has been their visits to the locales where I grew up and where their mother (my daughter) grew up. They have seen the house where I lived as a child when they visited my mother-in-law in Mississippi (who still lives in the house where James grew up). Then earlier this summer, they visited Hilton Head (where their mother grew up) and saw the first house she lived in there.

Actually, this experience of visiting the different areas where we grew up reflects the kind of 'mobile society' that's another example of changing family patterns. In generations prior to mine, most of the family stayed very close to the old home base. But for some time now the pattern has been for people to move to other locales that better suit their personal needs or desires.

So 'visiting the past' can be one way of bridging the differences between generations. Another is one that we just experienced yesterday. James and I, along with our daughter and three granddaughters, attended a major women's tennis tournament. We spent all day (seven or eight hours) watching tennis and just 'hanging out.'

This is relevant to the generational connection in that James and I grew up playing tennis for our local high school teams. Then he continued to play competitively in college, while I dropped out, only to return many years later to play in some 'over-45 tournaments.'

When our daughter and son were growing up in Hilton Head, it was quite a hotbed of tennis with a number of well-known tennis professionals in residence. So tennis was a big part of their lives, including both of them being 'ball-boys' for tournaments and both playing in a local league, with our son also playing for his high school team. And now all three of our

*Family*

granddaughters are taking tennis lessons, continuing the family pattern of enjoying this particular sport.

Of course, it doesn't matter whether it's a sport or a hobby or any other endeavor; what's important is to identify whatever common interests and activities exist within the family—and to reinforce those as part of your own special family pattern.

Another way we personally reinforce our close family connections is through a lot of inside jokes involving references to things only we can understand. Those quick references or knowing glances easily provide a small cocoon of closeness in the midst of any larger environment, reminding us that we are all part of this particular family.

\* \* \* \* \* \* \* \* \*

**Family Gatherings**                    November 2007

Many families gather together during this time of year. We just celebrated Thanksgiving in the U.S., and soon many cultures around the world will celebrate various religious holidays. In most instances, the celebrating is done with other family members. In fact, for many families this is the only time they all try to get together.

Most people look forward to seeing those in the family they haven't seen in awhile. And while having everyone all together offers special benefits, it can also be a drawback in being able to catch up with relatives on a one-on-one basis. Since it's difficult to continue to be close to people when you can't talk in a more in-depth, meaningful way than is possible in a large group, it takes a special effort to connect with each person individually.

I'm keenly aware of this issue due to what happened during most of the family gatherings of my family of origin when I was a young adult. We lived quite some distance from most of our relatives, so those trips home found me reverting to the same style of interacting that had been my habit growing up. Unfortunately, this meant that people didn't get a chance to know the updated me, only the version of me frozen in time from the past. And, of course, the same was true for me in failing to have an updated view of them and their lives.

After many years had passed, I began to feel that many of my relatives were strangers. My closeness to them was based primarily on the past, without really knowing who they were *today*. So I began making a concentrated effort to spend some time with each individual during those family visits. It was astounding to see the difference in the quality of these personal exchanges—and more importantly, the degree to which we were able to rebuild our connections.

One of the most dramatic examples of the benefit from this kind of one-on-one encounter was when I had an opportunity to spend a full 24 hours alone with one of my relatives. Since neither of us lived in the area where most of the family was based, about ninety percent of our interactions had been when we both visited our hometown at the same time. It had been difficult to spend much quality time together, but all that changed when I was traveling though the town where she lived and stopped to spend the night.

Frankly, I saw a side of her that I didn't even know existed. She'd always been the 'life of the party,' very talkative, and seemingly not very 'deep.' But during my visit, she showed me a very thoughtful, serious side that never came out in a group setting. Unfortunately, I never again had this kind of extended time alone with her, and I never saw that side of her again. But

I'm so thankful for the experience that allowed me to know her in this more complete way.

So as you come together with family members you haven't seen in awhile, I hope you'll avoid spending all your time with the whole group—or even with several people at a time. It takes some effort to carve out times for individual interactions, but there's a wonderful payoff in making that kind of commitment.

The total group time can be draining and sometimes stressful due to a clash of differing habits and preferences among the family members. But the one-on-one time is likely to be relaxing and meaningful, allowing you to look forward to family gatherings in a very different way.

\* \* \* \* \* \* \* \* \*

**Family Keepsakes** **December 2006**

I've spent the past few weeks going through all my boxes of family keepsakes. It's been a fascinating and touching experience that I thoroughly enjoyed.

I'd previously gone through all my old photos and passed them on to my kids at Thanksgiving. But going through the keepsakes was an even bigger job, particularly because there were lots of audio cassettes and it took a long time to listen to all of them. For instance, some were made when my kids were very young and singing silly songs, some were of my mother, and some were of my grandmothers.

I 'interviewed' my grandmothers when one was 85 years old and the other was 94. Many years ago I'd typed out copies of their words for everyone in the family and through the years had forgotten I still had the original tapes.

Some of the most touching keepsakes were those that my mother had left for me when she died, including my mom and dad's birth certificates and their marriage license—as well as their graduation diplomas from elementary school. They grew up poor in a very small town and married when Mother was 15 and Daddy was 17.

Since Daddy had to drop out of school to help support his family of origin and mother dropped out when they got married, the elementary school diplomas were the only diplomas they ever received—and proudly saved. So I'm passing them on, along with the inspiring story of how they made such a good life from such humble beginnings.

The keepsake boxes also contained many mementos of the special events from my own school days, some of which I particularly look forward to sharing with my grandchildren— like programs from my piano recitals and plays and information from some of my school yearbooks. It will also be fun to show them some of the cards their mother made for me when she was a child.

In fact, one of my granddaughters will be particularly pleased to see that a little picture her mother made for me when she was a child is almost exactly like the one my granddaughter made for me this past year.

Having done a lot of sorting through photos and keepsakes the last few months, I must say that it's been one of the most satisfying and grounding experiences of my life. It can be helpful to reflect on our past experiences as we chart a path through the rest of our lives.

\* \* \* \* \* \* \* \*

*Family*

## Mother's Day  May 2006

Mothers hold a special place in the heart of most people around the world. In the U.S. the phrase 'Mom and apple pie' signifies the essence of what people think of as *good*. And just think how many times you've watched a major sports event and seen some big brawny athlete look dead into the camera and use this opportunity to say, "Hi Mom!"

While Mother's Day is considered a very special day, all too often it's a symbolic day when people demonstrate the kind of love and care for their mothers that may be sorely lacking the rest of the year. So while it's nice to have a day to officially recognize the importance of mothers (and of fathers on their day), it's important to consider our relationship with our parents every day of our lives.

Since the death of my own Mother, my celebration of Mother's Day has been from the role of *being* a mother and grandmother. I feel a lot of love coming my way on Mother's Day. But far more satisfying to me is the love I feel from all of them throughout the year, not just on this one special day.

Even though my Mother died 18 years ago, in a strange way Mother's Day has a more powerful effect on my feelings about her than when we celebrated it together. I'm not sure why that is, but I think it has something to do with the tremendous sense of loss when you (selfishly) realize that you're no longer anybody's 'child.' (My Daddy had died much earlier, in 1971.)

Somehow it seems easier to fully appreciate your parents when they're no longer around. Our daily interactions with others invariably mean there are exchanges that we feel are positive and others we feel are negative. But when you no longer have the opportunity for *any* kind of exchanges, it's easy to recall only the best of our connection with them. So while I appreciated my parents before their deaths, I do feel I appreciate them even more now.

I hope that everyone who still has their mother or father with them will find it in their hearts to value the fact that they gave them life and forgive them for whatever parenting failures there may have been—either real or imagined. Also, we might keep in mind those who don't have mothers at all and would be eternally grateful for the opportunity to celebrate Mother's Day.

\* \* \* \* \* \* \* \* \*

**Special Memories**                                             **May 2006**

Today, May 18, is a special date in my family. My mother's funeral was held on this date in 1988—and this day is also my daughter's birthday.

During the years, I've often reflected on the circumstances surrounding Mother's death. Her death was actually a blessing, because she had suffered a tortuous series of debilitating physical traumas as a Type 2 diabetic, combined with heart problems and stroke. She finally died with gangrene.

But at this point I want to focus on the aspects of that situation that demonstrated the love and caring between these three generations of women—my mother, my daughter, and me.

I'd spent the last three weeks of Mother's life sitting by her bedside, never leaving the room for a minute. Even though she didn't know I was there, I felt a deep need to be with her, especially at the end.

*Family*

Since Mother lived in Mississippi (where I grew up) and I lived in California, I'd been away from my home during this three-week period. My husband had also been in Mississippi for the last week of this vigil, so our house had been closed up. After the funeral, I flew home—alone. (My husband had to go directly to a consulting job in another city.) When I changed planes on the way home, I was intent on finding *some* kind of birthday gift for my daughter. Fortunately, I was able to find a very nice cookbook in the airport gift shop that I knew she'd like, and I got it for her.

When I arrived back home, she and my son-in-law met me at the airport and took me home. When I entered the house, I could hardly believe it. My daughter had opened all the windows to air out the place, had put flowers in many of the rooms, and had spent the morning baking a cake in *my* oven—so that the wonderful aroma filled the house. I was overcome with the kindness, thoughtfulness, and caring she demonstrated with this loving homecoming. (After all, it was her grandmother who had died, and she was sad as well.)

Fast-forward to about 15 years later. In my daughter's presence, I was telling the story of how I had come home to find all the wonderful things she'd done to ease my return. My daughter looked at me with a very surprised look, saying, *"Mom, I don't remember any of that. What I remember about that day was how touched I was by the fact that in the midst of all you were going through, you made an effort to bring me a birthday gift."*

So each of us only remembered the kindness from the other—which is one of the reasons that this day stands out as special in so many ways. Special dates can be a reminder of what's important in life—and help us make the most of every day we have with those we love.

MUSINGS ON LIFE

\* \* \* \* \* \* \* \* \*

## Who You Gonna Call?   July 2007

No, not 'ghostbusters'—but family. We're fortunate to have a close-knit family where each member can call on the other for whatever help or support they might need. And we're particularly fortunate that the various areas of expertise of our son and daughter and son-in law are so varied—including the fields of law, medicine, and technology.

I recently had to call on my son for special tech help—and he came through for me in a wonderful way. He designed and developed my website 11 years ago, and through the years he trained me to handle most of the day-to-day functioning of the site. But I still turn to him whenever real technical expertise is required.

For instance, a couple of months ago we decided to add an integrated shopping cart to the site that included creating download pages on-the-fly. Since this was such a big undertaking (and since our son has a very demanding job as a Systems Administrator), we refused to let him take on this project. We knew a man who taught computer classes, including an upcoming class in shopping carts, so we hired him for the job. Unfortunately, it turned out that he didn't know as much as we (or he) thought, and after spending far more time and costing far more money than we'd anticipated, he became completely stymied and couldn't figure out how to finish it.

Here's where the 'Who you gonna call?' line became apparent. Naturally, we called our son. We apologized for not letting him do the job in the first place and asked him to take a look at it. While it entailed many aspects he'd never worked with before, he's a problem-solver and trouble-shooter, and he

*Family*

did it with flying colors. In fact, he did it 'from scratch,' using none of the work done by the previous computer guy.

While I'm very pleased with the look and the workings of the new shopping cart, I'm even more pleased at the fact that I have people in my life to call when I need help. I encourage you to pause a moment and consider who is *there* for you when you need them. Who in your life could you call on and be assured that their response would be like the lyrics from this old song by the Spinners?

*"Whenever you call me, I'll be there.*
*Whenever you need me, I'll be there.*
*I'll be around."*

\* \* \* \* \* \* \* \* \*

**Running with the Boys**                                              **June 2007**

I know nothing about horse racing, but like many young girls I was fascinated by horses as a child. And since my best friend lived on a farm and had a horse, I even got to ride occasionally. My only focus on horses through the years has been making a point of watching the Triple Crown Races.

This year, as usual, I watched all three of these races. The last one, the Belmont Stakes, was the most exciting race I've ever seen. While the Kentucky Derby was exciting because it was literally a 'photo finish,' the Belmont was even more exciting to me personally because I was invested in rooting for one particular horse, a filly named Rags to Riches.

She was the only 'girl' in the race, being up against a tough field of 'boys' made up of the best colts in the country—and she won. She also made history in the process, since it was the first time a filly had won the Belmont race in over a century! The last filly to win was in 1905, exactly 102 years ago.

It wasn't the horse race itself that meant so much to me; it's what it represented. I want my granddaughters to feel they can succeed at anything they want to attempt, regardless of the competition. They're already competitive in many areas—from academic pursuits to sports of various kinds, and they have a lot of confidence in their ability to succeed. But as they grow and try new things, they need all the confidence they can get, and any example like this can be helpful in sustaining their sense that 'girls' can do anything.

So I made a DVD of the race to show them the next time they come for a sleepover. Since they get a kick out of what they call 'girl power,' I can already anticipate the discussion that's sure to follow. It's not that I want them to be cocky or think they're better than others. But I know from my own experience (both personally and from my work as a corporate consultant on male-female issues in the workplace) that once young girls become women and go out into the work world, they often encounter situations where they're not seen as being fully capable of 'running with the boys.'

Since I have both a grown daughter and a grown son, I've always had a personal investment in both genders being able to reach their potential in all aspects of life. Our kids didn't appreciate it when they were growing up, but we made a point of seeing to it that both of them helped in the kitchen and cleaned their rooms—and both of them mowed the yard, etc. Until all our boys and girls view themselves as capable in all areas of life, we'll lose the benefit of the best each generation has to offer.

* * * * * * * *

*Family*

## The Soccer Generation             September 2006

This past weekend I attended three soccer games in one afternoon. (I have three granddaughters, and all of them participate in their local soccer leagues.) This soccer generation is fascinating to watch, which leads me to reflect on how much the times have changed.

I never heard of soccer when I was their age, growing up in Mississippi in the 40s and 50s. The 'big thing' was football (only for boys, of course), so I was a cheerleader. Then by the 70s when my own kids were soccer age, I was vaguely aware of one local team that played against other towns, but it was only for boys. So my daughter was a cheerleader—while my son loved tennis and played on the school tennis team. My daughter played tennis too, but not competitively.

But now that my granddaughters are sports age, they all play soccer. In fact, in this city, soccer seems to be even more popular among girls than boys. And between practices during the week and games every weekend (plus lots of tournaments), this activity dominates much of their time and energy. But they *love* it!

While I've always been interested in sports and understand the rules of most of them, I still fail to completely grasp all the nuances of the rules of soccer. But, of course, that doesn't keep me from thoroughly enjoying the game. And I'm gradually learning more about what's happening—beyond the obvious scoring of goals, which gets the most attention.

It's wonderful to see the girls so excited and committed to something that's also generally healthy for them—although I do worry as the older teams include 'heading' the ball as part of the game. Another concern is that they take it so seriously. But all in all, it's great to see the kind of teamwork and team spirit they all exhibit. In fact, I'm pretty sure that the team nature of soccer is one of the biggest drawing cards and most satisfying aspects of their involvement.

Of course, since tennis was my sport of choice growing up, I'm pleased that they also play tennis. However, soccer is clearly their first love in sports.

I do think it's significant that this generation of girls can choose to be involved in a contact sport, countering the idea that girls are weak or to be taken lightly. (In fact, one of my granddaughters particularly likes this aspect.) And I like the fact that it offsets the intense focus on girls' looks as determining their image of who they are and who they can be. So I anticipate great things from this new 'soccer generation' and am proud my granddaughters are part of it.

\* \* \* \* \* \* \* \* \*

**Children without Families**            **December 2007**

It's that time of year when children are excited about Santa and the toys they get for Christmas. But many children aren't concerned about this—because their wishes can't be granted by Santa. Their greatest wish is not for toys, but just to have a family to call their own.

While it's sad at any time to consider the number of children who don't have a 'real home,' it's particularly poignant at this time of year. I'm focused on this issue right now because I recently saw two movies depicting the stories of children without a home.

First, I went to a movie theater, where I saw "August Rush." This is the story of a boy who lived in an orphanage and had no firsthand knowledge of his parents, but who was

## Family

convinced that they would someday come to find him. It turned out that his father didn't know of his existence since his birth was the result of a one-night stand and the couple was separated by the woman's parents. As for the mother, she was told that the baby had died in a car accident she had while pregnant. Anyway, the child was so driven to have a family that he ran away from the orphanage in hopes of finding them himself. He succeeded through an unrealistic plot based on the fact that he was a musical child prodigy and both his parents were musicians—and they were drawn together through the music.

The week after seeing "August Rush," I watched another movie on TV that dealt with a similar theme, "Pictures of Hollis Woods." This was the story of a little girl named Hollis Woods who was passed from foster home to foster home, always creating problems and never finding the love and acceptance she craved. This movie also had an unrealistic plot involving the love of an Alzheimer's patient and a family who had lost a child of their own and finally convinced her to become part of their family.

In both movies, there was a 'happy ending,' but neither story was representative of what usually happens in the real world. My own lifelong interest in this issue comes from my personal experience when I was only 21 years old. My husband and I wound up serving as house parents in a children's home for about two years. The children we cared for were all boys between the ages of eight and twelve, and they were *not* orphans. They were children who had been placed in the home on a temporary basis because of the inability of their parents to care for them due to extreme poverty, abandonment or abuse. So while they were not technically orphans, their sadness and loss was in many ways just as difficult.

For instance, each Sunday was visitation day when family could come to visit. This turned out to be a bitter disappointment, regardless of whether or not anyone showed up. Those who had no visit from a family member were understandably disappointed, but those who *did* were invariably upset when the family member left again at the end of the day.

I hope that at this time of year (and, in fact, throughout the entire year) we remember the importance of caring not only for our own children, but for *all* children. Even if we can't do something directly for those children who are without families, we need to do a great deal more than giving lip service to the importance of children. We need to show by our actions, both individually and collectively, that taking better care of our children is one of our highest priorities.

* * * * * * * * *

**Happy 100th Birthday!** December 2007

My husband's mother was born on December 12, 1907, which means that she is now celebrating her 100th birthday. Naturally, this is a special event in the small town where she's lived almost all her life. Everyone (yes, literally everyone) in the town knows her—and loves her.

However, it's not just the local people who love her so much. Following the death of her husband more than 50 years ago, she spent several years as a house mother in a men's dormitory at the college where James and I had gone to school. Her gentle, caring nature led her to have an impact on these young men in a remarkable way. Many of them have stayed in

*Family*

touch with her through all these years, including periodically traveling to visit her.

Since James and I grew up together, I've known her all my life—and I can honestly say that I've never known a more thoroughly *good* person. I realize that a lot of people may be considered good, but it's quite impressive when you see someone whose entire lifetime is spent being kind, thoughtful and giving to everyone she encounters. No one has ever heard her say an unkind word about anyone! Frankly, I don't know anybody else about whom I could make that statement.

As we get older, we tend to more fully appreciate those in our family who went before us. This awareness can be particularly important if we try to learn from and emulate the best qualities of our ancestors. By trying to integrate some of the most admirable qualities of older family members, we can be stronger and more confident in facing whatever comes in our own lives.

For instance, although it's been many years since the last of my ancestors died, I have in many ways felt as close or closer to them than when they were alive. I think that's because I feel they are 'with me' in a different way now that there's no physical body to create separateness. And I've particularly felt their presence when facing life's difficulties in that I draw strength by reminding myself that I come from such strong stock.

Most of us will say "family is the most important thing in my life," but all too often our actions and our use of time don't reflect this sentiment. However, when people come toward the end of their lives (especially if they *know* they're nearing the end), most of them come to a greater appreciation of the importance of family. I think part of the reason is that the older we get, the more we think about the overall meaning of life—

and most of us ultimately find the most meaning in our families.

I hope that those who are spending time with their families during the holiday period will recognize that while not every family is going to have a 'Norman Rockwell' kind of time together, it's worth reflecting on just how fortunate you are if you're part of a loving family. It's also a good idea to put the appreciation into practice by telling the special people in your family how much they mean to you—before it's too late. Not everyone will have a wonderful family member who lives to celebrate their 100th birthday.

# Chapter 6: Character and Integrity

Character Assessment
Trusting your Intuition
The Power of Integrity
Strengths and Weaknesses
Your Net Worth
My Quest for a Wii
When Dreams Come True
Pressure to be Perfect
Winning and Losing
Telling the Truth

*Character and Integrity*

**Character Assessment**                              **August 2006**

All of us inadvertently reveal our true character in the process of going about our normal daily activities. That's because it's reasonable to extrapolate from the way someone acts in one instance to the way they're likely to act in other situations. This can be particularly useful when considering whether or not a specific person may be someone you would want in your life—as friend, colleague, or even acquaintance.

For instance, just this week I observed actions by people exhibiting both good character and quite questionable character. In one instance, I was standing in a long line at a checkout stand, just behind a person with a very large basket full of items. I happened to have only one item, but I wasn't in a hurry and wasn't showing any signs of impatience. However, the person in front of me insisted that I go ahead of them. This simple gesture told me a lot about the general nature of this particular person—that they tend to be aware of their surroundings and considerate of those around them.

On the other hand, I had another experience in a large crowded parking lot (where I'd been patiently waiting for a person to finish loading their purchases and back out of the spot) when another car from the opposite direction quickly sped up and whipped in the spot in front of me. I knew in a flash this was *not* the kind of person I would care to know or have as part of my life.

When you see people who are either oblivious or me-first in the way they move about, you get a pretty good sense of who they are as a person. The kinds of people I try to avoid are those who will do such things as park in a disabled spot when they're not disabled, break in line, or don't move over when meeting you on the sidewalk, causing you to step off the path.

While these examples are minor incidents with no significance in and of themselves, I've found that they generally reveal the typical ways people will behave in any situation. Of course, there are times when any of us may do things out of character, but more often than not, the way a person acts in one situation is representative of their basic way of making their way in the world.

While I personally value those people who are more thoughtful and considerate of others, I also recognize that many of us overdo it—which can create a whole different set of issues, particularly with long-term relationships of any kind. So it's important to apply the same consideration to ourselves that we do to others, trying to be as fair and straightforward as possible in all our interactions.

Even with the best effort, we won't always be understood or appreciated for our true character or for our efforts to interact in a straightforward way. For instance, back in the 70s when I did a lot of corporate consulting on male-female issues in the workplace, I did some assertiveness training for women. I found that I could teach women the appropriate words, tones and gestures to demonstrate assertiveness, but unless it fit with their internal sense of themselves, it didn't work. Overly-aggressive types tended to still behave that way, while overly-passive types continued in their preferred way of behaving.

Of course, there are many individual exceptions, but in general, men have been conditioned to be more aggressive and women to be more passive. But all of us would be better served by trying to simply exhibit the kind of character that would allow everyone to interact in an equal and straightforward manner.

In the meantime, it's good to know that people do provide lots of clues to their preferred way of interacting; you don't have to wait until you've placed too much trust in someone to find this out the hard way. Simply notice all their little insignificant acts as they go about their daily lives and you'll have a good indication of what to expect from them when the chips are down.

\* \* \* \* \* \* \* \* \*

**Trusting your Intuition**                                            **November 2006**

Nothing signifies our tendency to intuitively assess the character of others so much as the well-known question, "Would you buy a used car from this man?" While I just bought a used car from a woman, not a man, we generally need to ask ourselves the question, "How can you trust a person with whom you're engaging in any important transaction?"

Naturally, I wanted to check the car as carefully and thoroughly as possible in order to determine its reliability. But I recognized that I also needed to check my gut as to my feelings about the character of the person I'd be dealing with.

While I felt it might be safer to buy from a dealer as far as warranty, etc., I also realized that dealers normally charge a couple of thousand dollars more than an individual would charge for a comparable car. So I decided to explore both alternatives.

Looking at quite a few car dealerships, I encountered one seller with whom I felt quite comfortable, but I felt very uneasy about most of the others. I also checked out two cars that were 'for sale by owner'—and had two dramatically different experiences. One was extremely vague and deceptive while the other was like an open book.

The first car I looked at had a nice appearance and was offered at a very good price. I asked the owner a simple question, "How long have you owned the car and who did you buy it from?" She said she'd had it five months and bought it from 'the dealer.' I noticed it still had a tag from a local dealer, and asked if that's where she bought it. She said no, that this was just a temporary registration she'd gotten because she planned to move out of state and knew she wouldn't be keeping the car very long.

I wound up asking (in about four different ways) what dealer she bought it from, and she just kept saying 'the dealer.' So within the first five minutes, I instinctively knew that I couldn't trust buying the car from her. But I wanted to confirm my feelings, so I copied the VIN # and went home to look it up on CarFax. Sure enough, it was a 'salvage' car (having been wrecked) and there was a red alert about the car's condition as well as the ownership.

This experience almost soured me on even trying to look at another car from a private owner. But I found one listed on the Internet that sounded perfect, even being the color I wanted—not a condition, but a nice perk. After several emails and a phone conversation, my sense of the owner was extremely positive, so I decided to make the two-hour drive to go see the car.

Sure enough, both she and the car were 'quality' all the way. She was the original owner, had *all* the repair papers, and had babied the car beyond anything I'd ever encountered. She was only selling it because she was getting a new 2007 model. I felt from our earlier interactions that she could be trusted, but seeing her (and the car) in person made it crystal clear that she was a person of the highest integrity. Of course, I didn't go strictly on instinct; I'd already gotten the VIN # by email and checked the CarFax report to see that the car was just as she represented it.

Within a period of an hour or so (after driving the car and a little back-and-forth negotiation on price), I bought the car. I've had it for a week now—and it's everything I'd hoped.

This experience reinforced a mindset I've always had—that we can tell a lot about a person if we're willing to trust our instincts about their overall character.

\* \* \* \* \* \* \* \* \*

**The Power of Integrity**                                      **May 2007**

Lately, I've been thinking a lot about what characteristics provide an indication of a person's level of integrity. I'd like to offer some thoughts that I hope will help you increase your own effort to live a life of integrity—as well as to assess the level of integrity of others.

This is prompted by the continuous stream of news stories about politicians and business leaders who fail to speak up in a timely manner about things that impact a large number of people. Ironically, the information usually comes out later when they're no longer in office or no longer in positions of authority. Sometimes they voluntarily share information they had earlier withheld—and sometimes facts about their knowledge are exposed by others.

In any event, most of them (understandably) try to 'spin' their eventual disclosures to put themselves in the best possible light, despite whatever actions they took earlier. They seem to think that this vindicates their earlier behavior and redeems their integrity as a person. However, integrity involves a commitment to 'responsible honesty' about all important issues. (Note that 'responsible honesty' is more than 'not lying;' it's 'not withholding relevant information.')

Unfortunately, we sometimes think we have to bend the rules or cut corners in order to protect ourselves. We tend to 'go along to get along.' But we fail to appreciate the power in acting with integrity. That's because power doesn't depend on having the most authority, or the most information, or the most ideas, or the *right* answers.

'Position power' is not the only means of influencing others; another form of influence is 'personal power'—which is open to everyone. This personal power to influence others is directly related to being a person of integrity.

"What defines a person of integrity?"

A person of integrity is real, credible, genuine, and authentic. The bottom line is that you *know* a person of integrity when you see one. You recognize that they have the ability to get things done and to make a difference—based on their own personal power.

People of integrity can motivate others and instill confidence because there's no confusion about who they are or what they stand for. Especially when it comes to being able to influence others, people are energized not by credentials, expertise, or title—but by strength of character, integrity, and good will.

Integrity doesn't equate with being *good* or *nice*. Quite the contrary; it takes real courage to be a person of integrity. It involves:

—saying what needs to be said, whether or not it's popular.

—having no hidden agendas or ulterior motives.

—standing up for principles of fairness and equality.

*Character and Integrity*

—doing what's needed rather than what's self-serving or expedient.

So the next time you have that gut feeling that perhaps someone isn't operating out of a position of integrity, I hope you'll use the above guidelines to help determine the degree to which they can be trusted. The bottom line is that 'who you are speaks louder than what you say.'

Most of us have a general sense of 'who we are,' but much of the time that consists of identifying ourselves by our various roles (husband/wife, mother/father) —or by our jobs ('butcher, baker, candlestick maker').

But who you are is far more than the roles you play. As expressed in one of my favorite sayings, "A role is only a task. We've been using it as an identity."

\* \* \* \* \* \* \* \*

**Strengths and Weaknesses**                       **April 2008**

One of my strengths is that I'm a very good worker, perhaps too good for my own good—since this tendency also becomes one of my weaknesses when overused.

The definition of a workaholic is 'a compulsive worker.' That pretty much sums up the path I've been on the past few months. While I can be quite compulsive about a lot of aspects of my life, I become particularly obsessed when faced with a specific project. And I'm in the midst of a very big project that has led me to be a workaholic on steroids.

The silly part of my workaholism is that I'm my own boss and set my own schedule. Naturally, those who care about me encourage me to slow down, but I can't seem to rest when there's a big project sitting there to be done. It's not as if I can set it aside to pursue other things; I wind up carrying it around in my head whenever I try to do anything else—even sleep! Of course, the pressure I put on myself tends to tire me out and leave me functioning only on adrenaline, which no doubt diminishes my productivity.

I'm not proud of this compulsion to work like a fiend, so I've been trying to determine why I'm so driven to behave this way when I know it's not smart. One factor is that for most of us, our weaknesses often come from overuse of our strengths. While one of my strengths is an ability to bring a lot of focus and energy to situations that require this kind of attention, it becomes a weakness when I use it in situations that *don't* require this kind of effort. Unfortunately, I seem to have only one speed—full throttle.

Another factor in my case is the fact that I was raised to value hard work and sacrifice. Part of my sense of worth was developed based on the idea that it's important to 'finish your work before you play.' While I take pride in having a good work ethic, I've clearly taken it too far—to the point that this potentially positive asset becomes a liability when used inappropriately.

As often happens with these self-reflections, I don't have a clear solution to the dilemma. But I think the first step to changing anything about our behavior is first recognizing it, then acknowledging it (owning it), and finally *wanting* to change. So this is my challenge—to continue working on really wanting to make it happen.

I do this personal sharing to invite you to think about your own strengths and weaknesses—and whether, like me, some of your weaknesses may be due to overuse of your strengths.

\* \* \* \* \* \* \* \*

*Character and Integrity*

**Your Net Worth**                                **November 2007**

I've had a love/hate (mostly hate) relationship with money my entire life. Like most people, I want to have *enough* money—which begs the age-old question, 'How much is enough?' Most people seem to find that what they *need* is always slightly more than whatever they have at the moment. But I've never really aspired to *more*—and have, in fact, been quite uncomfortable with any dealings related to money. This has led me to give away a lot of my time and energy and in turn to find myself without the kind of security that money is supposed to provide.

Fortunately, many years ago, I addressed the 'security issue' by identifying with a quote I read saying, "Security is having more—or needing less!" So my tendency is to find ways to need less rather than to have more.

I think some of the reason for my feelings about money relate to the way I grew up, with very little in the way of monetary comforts.

Daddy was the oldest boy in a family of nine and had to drop out of school to help support his family of origin. Daddy worked very hard his entire life, spending many years working in a stave mill and finally getting a service station when I was 16 years old. As a consequence of my upbringing, one of my strongest values in life is to work hard and to be self-sufficient.

Another influence was the way Daddy was so generous with what he had, leading me to be more compassionate toward those who have very little. Unfortunately, I tend to be much less so toward those who have a lot in terms of 'things.'

I'm not proud of this bias, so I work to overcome it by reminding myself that all people face difficulties in life, regardless of their financial status. I'm convinced that if we could know the full life circumstances of those who *appear* to 'have it all,' we'd find that they also deal with many difficult challenges and deserve our compassion and understanding.

I share this as a way of pointing out how easy it is to judge people by outward signs (like money) while failing to see the *person* behind the image. It's important to avoid making a judgment about others on any standard other than their humanity. As the main song from the enormously popular "High School Musical" says, 'We're all in this together.'

This is particularly true when it comes to recognizing the temporary nature of not only our financial station in life—but life itself. We might be well served to keep in mind that when we come to the end of our life the final determination of our net worth will not be based on our finances. What will count is not how much money we had, but who we were and how many people's lives we touched. In that way, everyone has the opportunity of having a significant 'net worth.'

\* \* \* \* \* \* \* \*

## My Quest for a Wii                    December 2006

Shopping for hard-to-find items (especially gifts at the holiday season) can bring out both the best and the worst in people. This past week has been just such an experience for me—in my quest for a Wii. If you haven't heard of the Nintendo Wii, it's a new game system that's interactive in a special way that involves significant physical body movements. For instance, it has a package of sports games (including tennis, baseball, golf, bowling and boxing) that requires moving your body to control the action.

Anyway, a member of my family and I planned to go in together to purchase a Wii for another member of the family. And since my time was more flexible than the other person's, I was the one who embarked on this quest. I'd never had this kind of experience—and frankly, wound up finding it quite an adventure!

It began with a long wait outside a store that had advertised a 'guaranteed supply of 12 or more.' (I just missed out by a few people in front of me.) Then each day for the next five days, I checked with two or three stores and called many more, trying to determine the most likely prospects.

What I found was that some clerks were very brusque—understandably, perhaps, because they were constantly getting bombarded with questions as to when they'd get some Wiis in stock. I also found a good bit of duplicity—in that one store said every day for four straight days that they'd have some this week, then announced that they'd gotten them in, but wouldn't be putting them out until the weekend.

All this driving and waiting for stores to open (and then being disappointed) took a toll. I became pretty stressed out—to the point where I began taking a copy of a book I read a few years ago to read again each day while I waited. Appropriately, it was "Don't Sweat the Small Stuff"—and it did help.

The experience wasn't all negative, however. I also found some clerks who went out of their way to be helpful, even suggesting other stores that might have some in stock. But in the final analysis it took some real sleuthing work to put together the various pieces of the puzzle to figure out the best place and the best time to show up.

I also made some 'friends among strangers' with a few of the other regulars who went to the same stores I frequented. We formed a special kind of connection, sharing whatever each of us found out about availability at various places, even sharing phone numbers so we could alert others when we actually found a store with the Wii in stock. This reminded me just a little of the reports I've read about people who developed a special bond with others involved in some much more serious situations—like survivors of a plane crash, etc.

Finally, this morning, all my time and effort paid off—and I succeeded in my Quest for a Wii! And I just got a report from one of my fellow seekers that my telephone tip paid off—and they got a Wii also. While I often wished I had succeeded on my very first try six days ago, I also feel a certain satisfaction in having engaged in this quest—and in succeeding despite the odds.

If there's a moral to this story, it may be that patience, persistence, and forming good connections with other people can allow us to succeed at almost any challenge we may face.

\* \* \* \* \* \* \* \* \*

### When Dreams Come True                June 2007

I want to begin with a confession: I don't like opera. Even though I took piano lessons for twelve years, playing the classics, I somehow find listening to opera to be a grating, nervous-inducing experience. All that changed in an instant when I watched a man's dream come true on a talent contest in the UK. He sang opera in a way that thrilled me, inspired me, and gave me goosebumps.

His name is Paul Potts, a 36-year-old shy man who was working as a mobile phone salesman. He'd sung all his life, but hadn't been able to break through as a professional singer. His confidence was extremely low, having been bullied as a child and never gaining any self-esteem. His circumstances continued to be discouraging as he went through a long illness and incurred very large debts. After much hesitation, he finally decided to enter the contest—with no expectation that he would make it beyond the first round.

However, from the moment he opened his mouth to sing, it was clear that he was not only good, but perhaps the best opera singer ever. In fact, a friend of mine who has seen all the 'greats' in person says there's no question that Paul is the best!

So now he has a chance to completely change his life, since he's already recording an album for Simon Cowell's company (whom Americans know from American Idol). In fact, it was a special treat to see a hardnose like Simon be so surprised and impressed with Paul's talent. And as Paul began to sing for the first time, you could visibly see the woman judge on the panel literally have her breath taken away. But the audience reaction was the most moving of all as they broke into spontaneous applause after only a few bars of his first song.

In a time when there's so much bad news in the world, it's wonderful to be inspired by a positive, uplifting story like this. So even if you've already seen this story on the news, I hope you'll periodically watch his performance on YouTube—just as a reminder that occasionally dreams do come true.

\* \* \* \* \* \* \* \* \*

**Pressure to be Perfect**                                                   **January 2008**

I've been watching a lot of football lately—which I do only near the end of each season during the Bowl Games and the NFL Playoffs. I grew up in a small Southern town where football was a big deal, even being a cheerleader one year; so I learned to enjoy the game very early in life.

Anyway, much of the attention this season has understandably been on the New England Patriots—and their 'perfect' season. They're in the midst of the playoffs now, so I can only speak to the fact that they had a perfect *regular* season. It's too early to know whether they'll 'go all the way.'

But the pressure on that team as it approached it's last regular season game, going for a perfect 16-0 record, set me to thinking about how much pressure is involved for anyone who tries to be 'perfect' in *any* area. While we may see this more often in sports, it's also true in many other walks of life.

For instance, students who typically make A's often feel a lot of pressure to make Straight A's so they can have a perfect 4.0 (or above). Or older employees may take pride in having perfect attendance at their place of employment. And even beyond the measurable/quantifiable ways to determine perfection, many of us aspire to being perfect parents or even perfect friends—always there for those who count on us.

All this striving can take a toll. One of the reasons so many people experience debilitating stress and/or depression is because of the internal pressure we put on ourselves to be exceptional in whatever we do. The idea of being 'good enough' is a very difficult concept to embrace when we see how much praise is heaped on those who are 'perfect.'

Of course, some people may be 'slackers' and not care about trying to achieve anything special, but most of us feel some pressure to excel. However, we'd be better off if we could fully accept that there will always be others who are better than us in various ways—just as there will always be others who are less successful in some particular area.

## Character and Integrity

To be completely honest, while we admire those who seem to have achieved a level of perfection, we also tend to resent them because they may lead us to feel worse about ourselves. However, we could just as reasonably feel compassion for them. That's because I've never met a person who was extraordinarily successful who didn't pay a high price for the time and effort they devoted to striving for perfection in some particular area of their lives. Invariably, they had to give up something else (make a significant trade-off) in order to excel in their chosen area.

But even if the individual feels fine about their personal choice of trade-offs, it's often their families who pay the bigger price. For every highly successful person there's almost always someone else close to them who has 'taken up the slack' or 'taken a back seat' in order to make their success possible.

So the next time you're tempted to feel envious or inadequate or any kind of negative feeling related to someone else's seeming perfection, it's wise to remind yourself that all success comes with a price—and it might be a price you wouldn't really want to pay.

\* \* \* \* \* \* \* \* \*

**Winning and Losing** February 2008

I was one of the 93 million people who watched the 2008 Super Bowl game between the New England Patriots and the New York Giants—which set me to thinking about the whole issue of winning and losing.

Most of us have heard the famous sports quote, "Winning isn't everything; it's the *only* thing." While in sports it's important (even essential) to focus on winning and to strive to win, this sets up a serious challenge in appropriately handling the situation when you *don't* win—particularly if you're *expected* to win. This is what happened to the Patriots in their stunning loss to the Giants.

In the midst of all the understandable excitement by the Giants and their fans, there was one glaring example of how the 'winning is everything' mentality can lead to very unfortunate actions. Bill Belichick, coach of the Patriots, left the field with one second left in his team's loss to the Giants—thereby snubbing the Giants coach, Tom Coughlin, by avoiding the midfield congratulations that are an expected part of this whole ritual.

This was classic 'sore loser' behavior, but it was not the first time this particular coach had shown such disdain. After the 2007 Super Bowl (in which his team was defeated by the Indianapolis Colts), he snubbed the Colts quarterback, Peyton Manning. When Peyton approached him after the game, he turned and walked away, leaving Peyton hanging. And earlier in that 2006-2007 season he had snubbed Mangini after the Jets defeated the Patriots in Week 10. However, he smiled and shook Mangini's hand when the Patriots ousted the Jets in the first round of the playoffs.

Belichick's behavior has been the subject of a lot of analysis and commentary. Here's a quote about him from a Blog on SportsProf.com:

> *"But how you celebrate isn't really the measure of a man, is it? All of us can be great guys in victory, because that's pretty easy to do. What's much more difficult is how we handle defeat and disappointment, and what we do to rebound from it. Our leadership is measured, in part, on how we handle the difficult situations in life, such as losing."*

And here's the opening line from an article about Belichick in Newsday:

> "Sometimes a man's character, if not his whole life, can be encapsulated in the blink of an eye."

Despite the above focus on the behavior of Bill Belichick, that is *not* the point of this column. The significance of focusing on his behavior is to draw attention to the need for all of us to monitor our own attitudes and behavior when it comes to winning and losing. While we may not be involved in sports, there are countless ways in which each of us competes in one way or another. And while winning is preferable to losing, we don't want to lose our integrity in the process.

We also need to encourage our children to adopt a more balanced attitude toward winning and losing. Many young people are involved in sports today, and it's important to not only teach them the game—but to teach them about good sportsmanship. Everyone faces losses of different kinds throughout their lives, so learning how to deal with loss is as important as learning how to win.

\* \* \* \* \* \* \* \* \*

**Telling the Truth**                                      **February 2008**

Most of us believe it's a good thing to 'tell the truth.' In fact, in the U.S. our stated priority on telling the truth is quite clear.

*"We hold these truths to be self-evident, that all men are created equal..."*
—Declaration of Independence

*"Do you promise to tell the truth, the whole truth, and nothing but the truth?"*
—Oath required prior to testifying in U.S. courts

Generally, we think of 'the truth' as being a *fact*. (One definition says the truth is 'being in accord with fact or reality.') However, one person's view of the truth may not be the same as that of another person—even when reporting on the same facts. This is often seen in court when there are differences in the sworn testimony by different eye-witnesses to the same event. The reason for the different versions of the truth is that everyone has their own set of filters through which they see the world.

While we clearly place a high value on telling the truth, there's an interesting twist to this truth-telling in the way a growing number of people (particularly celebrities) have been stepping forward to tell the truth about their lives. Much of the time, the truth they disclose is far different from the image they'd projected prior to this truth-telling.

The most recent example is Valerie Bertinelli—child star of the TV series "One Day at a Time," later married to rocker Eddie Van Halen for 26 years. In her memoir she debunks her image as the wholesome girl next door by disclosing her experiences with drugs and affairs. She connected this desire to tell about her life with her recent 40-pound weight loss and "gaining my life back." This kind of thinking may partly reflect the belief as stated in the Christian Bible that "The truth shall set you free."

While telling the truth to the world at large may be problematic, telling the truth to the primary people in your life is an important requirement for having a quality relationship. Otherwise, we can't truly know each other in any real way. But truth-telling always needs to be done for the purpose of building and maintaining a close connection with someone else, not as a way of unloading or unburdening our secrets just to 'get them off our chest.'

## Character and Integrity

So I hope you'll consider just how truthful you are with those closest to you—and what you can do to share more of your own truth in a responsible way. We're often afraid to tell the truth for a variety of reasons. But while it's easy to see the risks in telling the truth, we often fail to see the risks in *not* telling the truth. Secrets kept from those you care about serve to create barriers to the degree of closeness that's possible in the relationship.

But when truth-telling is specifically for the purpose of sharing yourself (not criticizing others) and being truly known, it's likely that the truth really will set you free—free to have a stronger relationship than would otherwise be possible.

# Chapter 7: Communication

The Power of Words
Parent—Child—Adult
Ignoring the Elephant in the Room
Debating vs. Discussing
Everybody's Talking

Communication

## The Power of Words          September 2007

As children, most of us heard the saying: *"Sticks and stones may break my bones, but words will never hurt me."* Most of us also know that this is not true; words can be extremely hurtful. In fact, they can affect the way we see ourselves—and the way we see the world. This is especially true of words that are spoken to children when they're still forming their sense of themselves and their place in the world around them.

I was reminded of this recently when I witnessed a mother 'disciplining' her child in a public place. The harsh words she spoke to the child made me cringe. Frankly, I see less of this kind of display of anger than I did in years past, but it's still quite disturbing. It also led me to look among my keepsakes to find a poem from my grandmother that speaks to this issue.

My grandmother was the first to impress upon me the importance of our use of words. Beginning when I was a child and continuing until her death when I was 45 years old, she repeatedly recited a poem that she had learned as a child herself. At the age of nine, she'd memorized this poem and presented it to her class. Her memory was amazing in that she continued to recite it until her death at age 95.

Keep a Watch on Your Words
Poem spoken by Lizzie Barnett (author unknown)

*Keep a watch on your words, my children,*
*for words are wonderful things.*

*They're as sweet as a bee's fresh honey;*
*like the bees, they have terrible stings.*

*They can bless like the glad morning sunshine,*
*and brighten a lonely life.*

*They can cut the strifes of anger
like a cruel two-edged knife.*

*Let them pass through your lips unchallenged,
if they be true and kind.*

*If they come to support the weary,
to comfort and help the blind.*

*If a bitter, revengeful spirit prompt the words,
let them be unsaid.*

*They will flash through a brain like lightening
or fall on a heart like lead.*

*If they're cold and cruel,
keep them back under bar and lock and seal.*

*The wounds they make, my children,
are always slow to heal.*

*May peace guard your lives,
and ever from your early youth...*

*May the words you daily utter
be the beautiful words of truth."*

While the mother I witnessed verbally abusing her child didn't use *physical* punishment, that form of abuse often goes along with a willingness to resort to verbal abuse. So I'm concerned that a mother like the one I saw verbally abusing her child in public may treat her child even worse in private—not only with worse verbal abuse, but with physical abuse as well.

*Everyone* who deals with children needs to consider the ramifications of letting harsh words (or misguided efforts at discipline) affect the way you react to a child. And a good place to begin, as my grandmother said, is to 'Keep a watch on your words.'

*Communication*

Of course, it's not just children who are impacted by the words directed toward them. We may think as adults that we can exchange harsh words with other adults without harm. However, at some deep level, it hurts each of us—whether we're the one saying or hearing those words.

Ironically, we often use our kindest words in communicating with acquaintances, co-workers or strangers—saving our harsh words for those closest to us. I often refer to songs, and this is another instance where a song captures an important sentiment. In this instance, it's an old Mills Brothers song that begins, "You always hurt the ones you love. The ones you shouldn't hurt at all."

I hope you'll think of that the next time you're tempted to say something hurtful to someone, particularly the ones you love.

\* \* \* \* \* \* \* \* \*

### Parent—Child—Adult                              May 2008

Each of us has (at least) three parts to our personality; one part is our Parent, another is our Child, and the third is our Adult. This is a concept taken from Transactional Analysis (T.A.), and it can be extremely useful when trying to communicate effectively—particularly when dealing with the important people and issues in our lives.

If you're turned off by 'communication techniques,' I want to assure you that I intensely dislike most of them myself. For instance, I tend to be irritated by techniques that use phrases like 'I hear you saying…' At the same time, I realize that we're always going to have misunderstandings and disagreements with others, requiring that we be smart about the way we communicate.

A recent incident required that I be as careful as possible in the way I communicated, leading me to turn to T.A. as a tool for communicating more effectively. I used my T.A. understandings to help calm myself down so I could talk in a problem-solving (Adult) state rather than in a judgmental (Parent) state or an emotional (Child) state.

I can vouch for the power of these concepts—because I've used them during almost every major 'crisis conversation' I've ever had. (The times when I failed to use them were the times when things went downhill fast.) T.A. can be helpful in any situation where you want to be as effective as possible with your communication.

Below are some of the basics about Transactional Analysis:

T.A. is based on understanding that all of us have the capacity for three different ways of viewing the world and the events in our life.

1. We can view them from the Parent part of ourselves—based on being critical and judgmental. (The Parent style is based on the rules and values we were 'taught' by our parents.)
2. We can view them from the Child part of ourselves—based on being emotional and supersensitive. (The Child style is based on the impulses and emotions we 'felt' when we were very young.)
3. We can view them from the Adult part of ourselves—based on rational thinking. (The Adult style is based on facts and information we have gained through rational 'thought.')

Note that the Adult style takes into account the judgments of the Parent and the emotions of the Child, but filters all that through the rational, problem-solving part of ourselves. As much as possible, we want to integrate all three. In other words, we don't try to deny our judgments or emotions, but we try not to be *controlled* by them.

The way we exhibit the Adult style is not only through the words we use (fact-based, rational, problem-solving words), but also through our tone of voice (calm and even) and even our body language (attentive, thoughtful, confident).

It may seem overwhelming to remember all these guidelines, but the simplest way to get in touch with the Adult part of your personality is to reflect on the style most people use in business situations. Learning to apply some of those skills in your personal life can go a long way toward getting the kind of results you hope for in communicating with the important people in your life.

For anyone who wants to learn more about T.A., there's a 25th Anniversary Edition of the best book ever written on this topic, "Born to Win" by Muriel James. If you can't find it in bookstores, it's available through Amazon.com.

* * * * * * * * *

**Ignoring the Elephant in the RoomApril 2008**

I've had two separate experiences recently where there was a tacit understanding about 'ignoring the elephant in the room.' By that I mean ignoring some issue that's obvious, but that is *not* being discussed. For someone like me (who is honest to a fault and will talk about anything, anytime with anyone), this can be very difficult. But that's not everyone's cup of tea.

For instance, I remember once when a dear friend was obviously dying, his family chose not to openly acknowledge this fact. After he died, I felt sure there would be regret at not having addressed it earlier, but that was not the case. The family was still quite satisfied with having ignored it.

After many more such instances, I've finally come to recognize that not everyone feels the same about discussing important experiences or events. So I've accepted that even when you disagree with their choice, each person has the right to decide when they're ready to acknowledge something (even to themselves)—and certainly when to discuss it with others. So if they're not prepared to discuss it, they certainly don't want others to try to force them to do so.

It can be very difficult to stand by and watch this kind of situation, but they *do* have the right to refuse to talk about their own personal issues or experiences. This can happen for a number of reasons. Sometimes it's simply a coping mechanism in that they're doing the best they can at the moment. So it may be a matter of timing—of just not being ready to discuss a particular issue. At other times, they may *never* be prepared to confront 'the elephant in the room.' No matter how we explain the differences, each 'side' of this equation can find it frustrating to deal with the other.

So it's important to come to some level of acceptance of our differences on this matter. For my part, I've arrived at a very subtle distinction that allows me to feel more comfortable with ignoring some obvious issues. That happened only when I realized that it's not as if we're pretending the elephant isn't there. We all *know* the elephant is there—but have tacitly agreed to ignore it.

This may seem like a small point, but it makes a tremendous difference to me in that it keeps me from feeling 'fake.' That's because I'm not really pretending not to notice the elephant. I'm just respecting that the person who owns the elephant knows I see it and prefers that I ignore it.

So the next time you feel compelled to impose your preferences (no matter how strongly you believe they're the *right* ones), stop and think whether you have the right to try to force your point of view. It's really up to the person who owns the elephant to make that decision, whether or not you agree or understand their choice.

\* \* \* \* \* \* \* \* \*

**Debating vs. Discussing** May 2007

I've been watching some of the political debates for the 2008 U.S. Presidential election. And even though these are highly structured and supposedly designed to inform the public, I find the whole debate environment to be somewhat unsettling. Of course, debates are not restricted to these kinds of formal political debates; they're extremely prevalent on TV with the many programs where 'debate and confrontation' is the preferred format.

I find it even more unsettling when a confrontation affects me personally—as happened recently. While I was not personally involved in the debate, I have a vested interest in an organization where I recently witnessed an unfortunate situation when *discussing* a particular issue quickly led to *disagreeing* about it, and soon to all-out *debating* it. As often happens, especially if someone is losing the debate on the merits of their argument, it turned into a series of personal attacks—with people jumping in on both sides of the argument. At that point, all is lost because rational discussion has been replaced with emotional reactions.

I've always shied away from debating anything with anyone, especially when it comes to any 'hot-button' issues like politics or religion—where opinions can be very strong and intractable from every side. While I've been able to avoid debates about such issues, I've often been pressed to participate in debates on TV or radio about issues related to marriage or relationships—and I have always declined.

Debating is just not my style. I much prefer to simply state my opinions and let others do the same. I accept that others have different opinions and have adopted a 'live and let live' approach. However, if pushed to acquiesce to someone else's way of thinking, I can be very forceful in insisting that they back off. I prefer to simply 'agree to disagree' because I don't think people are convinced of an opposing position through debating the differences.

That's not to say that I don't think people can change their positions, even on some very deep issues. This has happened to me in a number of areas where my current thinking is completely different from an earlier point in my life. But I believe that change takes place best when we're simply exposed to open discussions of all kinds of issues and have the opportunity to gradually contemplate how our beliefs/opinions hold up under this kind of internal scrutiny.

\* \* \* \* \* \* \* \* \*

**Everybody's Talking**                                             **April 2008**

If you've heard me speak, you know that I talk *very* fast. In fact, most people are surprised that someone with a Southern accent can talk so fast—since the typical Southern speech

## Communication

pattern is much slower. I talk this way whether I'm talking with only one person or making a speech to a large audience.

Actually, I've received repeated suggestions to slow down when I'm making speeches. But I've always resisted, knowing that it's not critical that people hear every single word I say. It's far more important that they get the overall sense that I'm overflowing with information—which helps sustain their interest and can motivate them to want to learn more about the issues I'm discussing. So my preferred style of talking is fast—and in person.

Of course, everyone has a preferred way of communicating, and more and more that seems to be electronically. Email and cell phones have become extremely popular modes of communication—even when in the presence of others. It's not uncommon to see someone on their cell phone or blackberry while another person waits patiently for them to complete their conversation. It's also not unusual to see two people together in public—with each of them talking to someone else on their cell phones.

It sometimes seems that everybody's talking all the time. And with the younger generation, this *talking* primarily takes the form of text messaging. In fact, these young people often carry on several conversations at once. When in their presence, they may be talking to you while carrying on one or more text-message conversation at the same time.

Most people today lead hectic lives and place a high priority on being able to multitask. This usually means that no matter what activity you're involved in, you're *also* engaged in some form of communication. And even when not actively talking, you're likely to be watching TV, listening to others talk.

There's been a gradual move toward being involved in almost constant communication, which is not likely to change unless people recognize that all this talking may come at a price. For instance, there's almost never time for quiet contemplation or reflection. And I wonder about the fallout from the lack of solitude in our lives. I wouldn't be surprised to see long-term problems resulting from the lack of occasional stillness in the midst of life's turmoil.

So as I try to slow down and stop the chatter in my own life, I invite you to consider what might help recharge your batteries as well. While we clearly need to continue talking with others, it can be draining if there's no time set aside to absorb or make use of all the information we're bombarded with every day. Like most things in life, balance makes all the difference.

## Chapter 8: Simple Pleasures

It's the Little Things
Seeking Happiness
Music Makes me Happy
Enjoying America's Pastime
Dog Days of Summer
Talking about the Weather
Desperately Seeking Nature
Vacation Time
What do you Enjoy?

*Simple Pleasures*

**It's the Little Things** July 2006

"It's the little things." This is a comment I seem to be making quite often these days. After years of seeking things in life that were *special*, I've now come full circle to a wondrous appreciation of 'the little things'—by which I mean the simple pleasures in life.

For instance, I've traveled a good bit and enjoyed some fine meals in very nice restaurants, but I find that my current favorite place to eat out is in a very simple outside plaza that serves only basic food like pizza, hot dogs, a few salads—and my favorite, frozen yogurt. In fact, we've developed a weekly ritual of going to this area to shop—and timing it so we have lunch in the plaza.

It's not the food that matters; it's the great people-watching. Like a lot of folks, I enjoy having a good location to just sit and watch the wide variety of humanity that strolls past, especially the children. But it's also fascinating to see the outlandish styles of (inappropriate?) dress that seem to be so prevalent these days. Frankly, you see a little bit of everything—the good, the bad, and the ugly. And I find it utterly entertaining.

But beyond the pleasures of the food and the people-watching is the pleasure of just sitting and talking for an hour—about non-serious things. All the serious stuff dominates our lives most of the time, so deliberately seeking out times to set aside the focus on work or personal problems or the state of the world at large can be a healthy way to bring more balance to our lives.

So even though my husband and I are together almost all the time (our desks with our computers are in the same room, we sit together to watch TV or read the newspaper, and we sit out back on our little patio and watch the rabbits in the evenings)…this weekly outing has become a ritual that we find particularly pleasant.

As with many of the simple pleasures in life, they're not calculated or planned in advance; they simply happen and then you notice how pleasant it can be and set out to repeat it. So it's important to notice when you find something simple that's also satisfying—and try to make more room for it in your life.

\* \* \* \* \* \* \* \* \*

### Seeking Happiness   March 2007

I've felt particularly happy the past week or so. I don't see myself as a typically happy-type person (and there's been no particular incident to account for this happiness), so I wondered what might have promoted these good feelings.

Finally I realized that much of it has to do with the fact that I've been enjoying some of the simplest things in life—outside activities like swimming and walking on the beach, being stimulated and motivated by hearing an exceptionally fine speech about child development, and not feeling quite as rushed and pressed for time as usual.

Most people want to be happy, and in the U.S. we tend to see happiness as our 'right.' (The Declaration of Independence declares that at least the *'pursuit* of happiness' is one of our rights.) But I suspect that *seeking* happiness is precisely the wrong way to actually find it.

For instance, some of our most prevalent expressions (like Happy Birthday or Happy New Year) relate to quite temporary, superficial events. This is a far cry from the official definition of happiness as 'a state of well-being and contentment.'

*Simple Pleasures*

This kind of happiness comes from within (from a way of being in the world), not from *having* something or *doing* something. In fact, happiness often comes from the simplest of life's pleasures—like noticing and enjoying a sunny day or a thing of natural beauty or the wonders of children, especially if the children are close to you.

One of the mysteries surrounding happiness is the way we see some people we think *should* be happy (like people with money, success or fame), only to discover that they feel extremely *unhappy*. On the other hand, we sometimes see people whose outward circumstances seem so dire that we think they *must* be unhappy, but they seem to find joy in the smallest pleasures of life.

This disconnect between absolute circumstances and their impact on individuals is due in large part to the fact that our sense of whether or not we feel happy has a lot to do with the gap between what we *expect* out of life and our actual existence. So people who expect little may feel happiness in small pleasures while those who expect a great deal may feel unhappy due to not having their expectations met.

Of course, there are many contributors to our individual sense of happiness, another one being the degree to which we are constantly analyzing our own happiness. Focusing on our own degree of happiness is not likely to produce good feelings. But thinking about how to make others' lives better can lead to happiness as a by-product of that focus.

Some would say the feelings from helping others reflect *satisfaction*, not real *happiness*. But I would argue that this way of thinking serves to distort the true meaning of happiness, which, as I said, has more to do with a deeper state of well-being than with a superficial state of pleasure or excitement. In fact, the letdown at the conclusion of any temporary period of excited activity can lead to feelings of far *less* happiness in the long run.

So I hope the next time you feel unhappy, you'll do a quick mental check as to how you're defining happiness. Are you defining it as a temporary high—or in terms of a more general sense of well-being? This awareness can be the first step to experiencing the kind of happiness that eludes efforts to actively seek it.

* * * * * * * * *

**Music Makes me Happy** May 2006

I'm not very good at having fun, being far too serious most of the time. But one of the things that has the ability to make me feel lighthearted is really good music. Therefore, I recently had a lot of fun at a local Blues Festival that also included Zydeco. If you're not familiar with Zydeco, it's cajun music—closely related to Blues.

I like a lot of different kinds of music, in fact, pretty much anything except classical—which is strange, since I studied piano for twelve years. But my very favorite is 'the Blues.' What I think is particularly interesting about the Blues is that it seems to be sad music, but I prefer to think of it as simply being full of soul.

I also love to dance, and this is one the few types of music where you see people of all ages out there doing their thing—and nobody cares.

Anyway, it makes me feel rejuvenated and ready to get back to my serious way of life. (You know the old saying, "All work and no play makes Jack/Jane a dull boy/girl.") So I really

*Simple Pleasures*

should 'get out' more often—because this kind of experience invariably makes me feel lighter, happier, and more vital.

I do hope that each of you reading this will think about what makes you feel this way—and determine to find a way to have more of it in your life.

\* \* \* \* \* \* \* \* \*

**Enjoying America's Pastime**                       **July 2006**

Last night I was again reminded of how it's the simple things in life that often bring the most pleasure. I'm usually reminded of this when I'm engaged with my grandchildren, seeing the world through their eyes.

But last night I enjoyed another child-like experience: going to a major league baseball game. Many years ago, we lived in Pittsburgh during the hey-day of the Pirates when they won the World Series in 1971. I used to really enjoy attending the games, but I'd forgotten how much fun it could be.

For instance, I've lived in San Diego for the past 20 years, but have only gone to a few games over the years, and I hadn't been at all since they built a new stadium a couple of years ago. So from the moment we arrived last night (I went with my son), I marveled at the terrific layout of the stadium. We got in on $5 tickets that allow you to stand at designated places all around the stadium—which was terrific. We stood part of the time directly behind home plate, but also went up to see the view from the nosebleed section.

Anyway, it was a very family-friendly place—with a grassy area to spread out on the ground and a special area with bleachers directly above a large sandbox where the children could play throughout the game. As I've said, people-watching is one of my favorite pastimes, and this was highly entertaining at the game last night.

Of course, it helped that the game itself was quite exciting. After a very slow start when the opposing team went way out in front with 4 runs, our team came back to tie it—then won in the bottom half of the 9th inning. That's about as good as it gets! Naturally, this was quite exciting, and I was spontaneously jumping up and down, clapping my hands, and yelling—like everyone else.

But it wasn't the winning that made it such a great night. I was thoroughly enjoying myself long before the final results could be predicted. It was the simple pleasure of letting go and having fun. As I've shared in the past, I don't do nearly enough of that—and, I'm afraid, neither do most of us 'responsible' adults.

So I hope you take time occasionally to do whatever brings you joy. And while being frivolous and irresponsible is not a worthy goal, it's quite important to include time for fun in our lives. It can bring more balance to our lives and make us more effective overall.

\* \* \* \* \* \* \* \*

### Dog Days of Summer — August 2006

According to the dictionary, the term, 'dog days of summer' refers to the period between July and early September when the hot sultry weather of summer usually occurs in the northern hemisphere. But another definition is 'a period of stagnation or inactivity.' Sure enough, all around us things have slowed down—a lot.

*Simple Pleasures*

Since I'm generally a pretty intense person and tend to rush through life, these warmer days do allow me to relax a bit more than usual. I think part of that is due to my sense of the overall slower pace of life at this time of year. For instance, most businesses are operating with a much smaller staff and at a much slower pace, most non-news TV programs are reruns of shows aired earlier in the year, and many people are taking vacations during these final weeks of August.

I'm not taking a vacation, but I particularly enjoy the 'dog days' because of my very strong preference for really warm weather. While others may complain about the heat this time of year, I must admit that I'm personally happiest when I can go around in short sleeves and barefooted. So these waning days of summer suit me just fine. (Of course, I also recognize there's a serious aspect to our current weather patterns due to Global Warming—which I discuss in the last chapter.)

I think my preference for warm weather is partly due to the fact that I grew up in the Southern part of the U.S. where the summers were very warm. And even though I now live in what is one of the more ideal climates (in Southern California), I would trade the perpetual spring conditions here for a little more hot summer. Actually, I can't complain about the weather here because it suits me so much better than the years I spent in much colder climes—13 years in New York, Connecticut, and Pennsylvania. In fact, I sometimes wonder how I made it through those times.

Clearly, this is one of my more frivolous columns, but I thought it seemed somehow appropriate to just lay back and talk about the weather, without trying to make it meaningful or significant—just going along with the spirit of the dog days of summer.

Of course, the pace of life will pick up again all too quickly, so we might as well enjoy this temporary break as much as possible and try to use it to recharge our batteries to be better prepared to address all the important issues we face in the world today.

\* \* \* \* \* \* \* \* \*

**Talking about the Weather** December 2006

The weather is one of the most popular topics of conversation. It's often used as an icebreaker (no pun intended) for casual conversations because it's seen as such a *safe* topic. However, weather can also be a very serious matter—and extremely influential in our lives.

Of course, natural weather disasters have the most dramatic impact—as clearly evidenced by the hurricanes, floods, tsunamis, and wild fires that have been so prominent in the news the past few years. Like most people, I'm concerned about all these natural disasters and the cost in terms of human life and property. I was also more personally impacted when my daughter's family lost their home in one of the wild fires that struck Southern California a few years ago.

Whether or not you've had a particularly difficult weather-related experience, weather strongly influences some people on a daily basis. For instance, I'm one of many people who find that the weather has a very strong impact on my mood. A warm, sunny day makes me feel positive, uplifted, energetic and happy. A cold, dreary day (especially if it's day after day of that kind of weather) can lead me to feel depressed and dissatisfied with life in general. I realize that many people are not strongly influenced by the weather, but those of you who

*Simple Pleasures*

do experience weather's impact on your daily moods know just what I mean.

Actually, just yesterday I was reminded of one of my worst experiences with bad weather when a friend of mine (who lives in a very snowy area) told me about her recent move into a new home during a snowstorm. Her story led me to recollect my experience of moving during freezing, snowy weather many years ago in upstate New York—while I had the flu. Frankly, it almost killed me. I went beyond what I *should* have done in moving—and wound up with a serious relapse, with the doctor ordering me to bed for two months!

So whether you're a snowbunny who loves the winter weather or a snowbird who's always chasing the sun, I hope you find a way to enjoy your experiences with the weather of your choice—and that you appreciate the days when you experience whatever you deem to be 'good weather.'

\* \* \* \* \* \* \* \* \*

**Desperately Seeking Nature** October 2006

I try to be responsible in taking care of my health and fitness, including regular visits to the YMCA where I spend time on the treadmill. But the treadmill is no substitute for walking outdoors—surrounded by nature. So James and I like to go hiking and explore new areas.

Some of our most enjoyable hikes have been in special places of natural beauty when we've traveled to Sedona, Arizona, or other locations offering different scenery. But we also enjoy hiking in areas near where we live in Southern California.

So last weekend we read about a trail near us that was described as being very beautiful and enjoyable. So we set out to soak up a little nature. The trail was two miles one way. It was not a loop, so you had to turn around and retrace the two miles back. The four-mile hike sounded about right for the amount of time and energy we were prepared to invest on that day, so we set out with great expectations.

Unfortunately, our hope of communing with nature was not to be. There was never a point along the entire hike when we were not within full sight of either a road or houses up on the hill. Also, the description included information about crossing a creek, but the creek had run completely dry and we saw only one place on the trail with a very tiny wet spot. Basically, it was not a trip into nature, and we could have just stayed home and walked around our neighborhood.

OK, so no big deal. However, our hope for the hike was not just to enjoy a pleasant view. It was for the much greater benefit to be had from the peaceful, calming effect that being out in nature can provide—to help offset the constant stimulation inherent in modern daily life.

The learning we gained from this experience was not just to be more careful about our choices of hiking locations, but to find ways to cut down on the amount of stimulation that leads us to feel the *need* for this kind of calming experience. Between our computers, cell phones and TV, most of us are constantly being over-stimulated, which is what sets us up for 'desperately seeking nature.'

۰ ۰ ۰ ✦ ✦ ✦ ✶ ✶ ✶

*Simple Pleasures*

**Vacation Time** July 2007

Fortunate are the people who can take an annual vacation. Not everyone can afford to take a vacation, and not everyone who *can* afford it actually does it. (Too many 'workaholics' these days.)

For many years James and I never took a vacation in the sense of going somewhere to sightsee or just relax. Since all our relatives lived in Mississippi (and we moved away from Mississippi almost 50 years ago), our vacation time was spent going to visit relatives. We felt it was important for us and for our children that we have regular contact with our extended families.

Although we couldn't afford to take additional time to *also* take a more traditional vacation, we never felt it as a loss, because during many of those years we lived in Hilton Head Island, SC—which is a vacation spot for many people.

Then when we left Hilton Head, we moved to the coast of Southern California, another place where people come for a vacation—again leading us to feel we didn't really need to go anywhere. So it took us a long time to appreciate that the importance of taking a vacation is not in where you go; it's simply in the fact that it's somewhere other than your normal environment.

We still rarely take vacations, but I now recognize that the break in the routine of daily responsibilities is the real measure of a vacation. I'm virtually never as relaxed at home with all the demands of everyday life as I am when we get away.

We do plan to get away for a few days later this month, and I'm having some misgivings about my plans this time. I'm setting it up where I may not experience the sense of freedom and relaxation that I so enjoy. That's because I plan to take my laptop computer with me—and now that it serves as the processor for my regular computer at home, I'll still have all my data and programs at my disposal during the trip.

So it's going to take some discipline to avoid continuing my work on the road the same as if I were still at home. I'm one of many people whose work is so integrated with their overall lives that it's hard to separate work time from free time. Since my focus is on writing and on working with my website, there are no hours that are clearly work hours and none that are clearly free hours. Unfortunately, this integration winds up shortchanging the free time—while the work time is filtered throughout each day.

I still fondly recall a period many years ago when I burned out from my independent work, and decided to take a job in a bookstore with regular hours. While the pay was extremely low, it was worth it in order to have a more ordered life for a few years. And being a bookaholic, I thoroughly enjoyed the work. But I particularly enjoyed the feeling of being 'off the clock' in the sense that when I was not working, my mind was not still a captive of the job. It felt incredibly freeing, a little like taking a vacation.

As I mentioned in the beginning of this piece, not everyone can afford to take a vacation. In addition, they may find no enjoyment in their job or they may work two jobs, never being able to take any time off. So those of us who are fortunate enough to be able to take a vacation might be more conscious of using it in a way that allows us to rejuvenate as a person. That way we'll be better prepared to come back to everyday life with renewed energy as well as a greater appreciation for the opportunity to have vacation time.

\* \* \* \* \* \* \* \*

*Simple Pleasures*

## What do you Enjoy? January 2008

It's time for the January Sales, which makes me happy—and reminds me once again how much it's the little things that can make a difference. Naturally, getting stuff on sale can make a difference in your pocketbook, but it can also make a difference in your mood.

For instance, my daughter was given a pair of warm fuzzy pajamas that were made from the softest, coziest material I had ever felt. (Actually, it felt somewhat like a pair of warm footies that I enjoy.) I'd wanted a housecoat made of this material, but felt it was too expensive, so decided I just wouldn't ever have one. But when I found out there were much less expensive pajamas made of this material, I went shopping for a pair for myself.

When I got to the store, I found that almost all these pajamas were gone—except for one pair that had been returned. They were not the right size (way too big), but I tried them on and never wanted to take them off. And the fact that they were on sale (for 70% off) sealed the deal. I was almost giddy at getting such a bargain. And that happy feeling has continued—as I sit here now on my first morning wearing the new pajamas. My husband kidded that he would have seen to it that I got these pajamas a long time ago if he'd known what a lift they would be to my spirits.

Of course, I don't expect this feeling to last indefinitely because there are too many important issues to be dealt with on an ongoing basis. But it does remind me of how much better we may be able to deal with the serious aspects of life if we also do things to remind ourselves of the simple pleasures in life.

The simple pleasures may be different for different people, but there are some basics that are available to most of us most of the time. Simple things like watching babies, feeling sunshine on your face, a warm bath or shower, the hug of someone you love, being out in nature, and dancing or other body movements that make you feel 'alive.'

So take a moment to reflect on what might bring you some simple pleasure—and thereby refresh you for returning to 'taking care of business.' One way to do that is to work through the following exercise from our LifeDesign Workbook:

*"List the 10 things you like to do most.*
*(Don't worry about order of priority)."*

PAUSE TO MAKE YOUR 10-ITEM LIST
BEFORE READING FURTHER

After making your list, then complete the rest of the exercise as follows:

*"Write down 'when' you last did whatever it is you like to do. Make a notation as to whether it was yesterday, two weeks ago, two months ago, two years ago, etc.*

*"If you're not getting around to doing the things you like to do best, you need to ask yourself why. And you need to determine what you're losing and what it will do to you over the long run if you continue this way. Life satisfaction usually depends on having a reasonable balance between responsibility and enjoyment. You're likely to pay a heavy price for letting either area dominate your life at the expense of the other."*

## Chapter 9: Health and Fitness

Let's Get Physical
Stress!
Killer Headaches
Getting a Good Night's Sleep
Age is Relative
The Common Cold—and Cancer
Breast Cancer Awareness
Living with Breast Cancer
Minor Surgery
What You Don't Know *Can* Hurt You
Modern Medical Advances
Losing my Mind

*Health and Fitness*

**Let's Get Physical**                      **September 2007**

I sit here tired—but happy. I've spent the past few days thoroughly cleaning the whole place and clearing the furniture to make way for a full carpet cleaning today. While I'm exhausted, I'm also quite pleased that I can still do this kind of intense physical work at age 71.

I've always prided myself on being physically capable of hard work. There's something about feeling you can 'take care of yourself' that feels good. Men generally have that feeling, but for women it's somewhat more complicated. Due to differences in physical strength, women are vulnerable in a number of significant ways, the most obvious being rape and physical abuse. But we may also see ourselves as less able to undertake physical challenges that have nothing to do with being vulnerable.

It's been satisfying to see the changes through the years in the way young girls see themselves in terms of their physical abilities. My own granddaughters demonstrate this every day, primarily through their commitment to sports. Team sports were quite limited when I was growing up, but today's young girls begin their sports endeavors very early, especially in the sport of soccer.

While it's nice if you began sports or other physical activity early in life, it's never too late to begin. I've read some remarkable accounts of people in their 60s and 70s who took up some new physical activity—and excelled! Of course, it's important to take care in how you go about any physical efforts. For instance, I had serious back problems about 20 years ago and try to sit, stand and move in ways that keep my back strong. And when I do particularly demanding work, I always wear a back support—just for insurance.

We ask a lot of our bodies, but often don't keep them strong enough to effectively respond to what we demand of them. And the older you get, the more critical it becomes to be able to continue calling on your body to function in a way that allows you to maintain your quality of life.

It's important to focus on what you can do to keep your body fit and healthy so it can continue to serve you throughout your life. You don't have to undertake an extremely vigorous set of activities. In fact, some of the most effective things you can do (like walking and stretching) require no equipment and can be done by anyone. For the past 20 years or so I've done a 15-minute stretching yoga every morning, and I walk almost daily. These simple activities have served me well.

By the way, this effort to maintain your fitness and physical strength is not just something you *should* do. There's real joy to be found in the feelings that come from getting physical. You move better, breathe better, think better, and sleep better. In fact, given all my physical exertion the past few days, I should sleep very well tonight.

\* \* \* \* \* \* \* \* \*

**Stress!** **November 2007**

I've been feeling particularly stressed lately. Actually, it's embarrassing to acknowledge the degree of stress I feel—because my life is so much easier than that of many others. But stress is not a direct result of what happens to us; it's due to our individual ways of *reacting* to the events and circumstances of our life.

Anyway, I've become aware that I need to start doing more of the things I know can be useful in dealing with stress. And I just got another motivation for doing this while watching a TV program about the book "You: Staying Young." Dr. Mehmet Oz, one of the co-authors of the book, said that stress is the single most important factor in aging. While I feel healthy and fit at 71, I do recognize that I need to take more seriously the threat of unaddressed stress.

Of course, everyone feels stress throughout their lives. Frankly, it's impossible to avoid—and stress is not *all* bad. That's because stress is not produced only in reaction to negative experiences, but to positive experiences as well. For instance, on the standard scale for assessing the stress levels of certain events, divorce is 73 and marriage is 50; both are stressful, with divorce only slightly more so than marriage.

To further complicate things, in addition to the kind of stress that's brought on by certain events, there's another kind that is a low-level, constant 'state of stress' associated with the hectic lifestyle that affects so many of us today.

Frankly, I've always been much better at dealing with a genuine crisis; I tend to stay calm in the face of a real emergency. But I generally do a terrible job of dealing with the stress of everyday, nitty-gritty, garden-variety issues that are a normal part of life.

As I've shared before, my own style is to do everything far too quickly. I tend to walk fast, talk fast, think fast, react fast—and generally rush through life. Of course, this style tends to increase stress levels on an ongoing basis. The irony is that although my schedule is fairly flexible, I actually impose schedules on myself. And once I commit to a certain project or effort, I get stressed out if I fail to meet my own self-imposed deadlines.

Of course, everyone feels stress and reacts to it in different ways, so each of us needs to assess our own personal way of generating (and dealing with) our stressful feelings. Naturally, it's better to avoid *negative* stressors whenever possible, but since some stress is inevitable, there are things we can do on an ongoing basis that can strengthen our ability to deal with it.

Basically, any activity that quiets the mind and relaxes the body can be helpful. That's why things like meditation, deep breathing, quiet time, good sex, gentle exercise, and relaxing music can help keep stress at bay—or at least help us deal with stress when it interferes with our lives.

It's smart to pay particular attention to how we begin and end each day. Most people are very rushed in the morning with the effort to get ready for the day. But some very committed people get up earlier than the rest of their family—just to have quiet time alone before things get too hectic.

I do pretty well with the way I *begin* each day, but I fail miserably at what's suggested for quieting down before retiring at night. Like many people, I tend to end the evening by watching TV. I'm discriminating in that I watch shows I've taped earlier in the day rather than just channel-flipping and watching whatever happens to appear. But any TV program serves to stimulate rather than relax us, making it much more difficult to recover from the stresses of the day.

My new resolve is to spend the last part of the evening listening to some relaxing music that I've had for some time but seldom use—or at least to turn off the TV well in advance of retiring. And I hope each of you will consider how you deal with the stresses in your own life—and determine how you can better prepare yourself to deal with them more effectively.

\* \* \* \* \* \* \* \* \*

*Health and Fitness*

**Killer Headaches** November 2006

It has now been two months since I've had any chocolate. I realize this sounds as if I'm at an AA meeting for chocoholics. But there's a big difference; it's not a lifetime ban on chocolate. I only have to go two more months before I can reintroduce chocolate into my diet.

The reason for avoiding chocolate (and many more of my favorite foods, including cheese, peanut butter, all fresh bread items, and almost every packaged food) is because this is part of an overall effort to rid myself of what I call 'killer headaches.'

Diet is only one aspect of the various 'triggers' that combine to put me above my headache threshold. Other factors include getting enough sleep and avoiding undue stress. But diet is a *major* factor that I only recently learned about—and it makes a huge difference.

I'd been having really severe headaches about every other day for several months. But since I started this new regime a couple of months ago, I've only had one bad headache. The plan is to continue avoiding all the trigger foods for a total of four months, then add them back (one per week) to test to see which ones are specific triggers for me.

I've been on a variety of diets during my lifetime, and there has always been an issue with willpower and discipline. But even though this one is much more restrictive than anything I've ever done, I have absolutely no resistance to strictly adhering to the guidelines. That's because it's not like other diets where you have to wait for the results. The feedback on this diet is immediate. If you adhere to it, you avoid headaches; if you don't, you have a headache. This makes it *very* easy.

As with many aspects of life, the common wisdom is not always the best. Like many people, I spent years taking various over-the-counter pain medications. But I've learned that all this does is set up a rebound headache once the medication wears off—and then you're right back where you started.

So I consider this sharing to be a public service for those of you who suffer from severe headaches. (Naturally, you should check with your doctor first—which I did also.) But if you want to learn more about this approach to controlling headaches, I recommend a book by Dr. David Buchholz of the Johns Hopkins University School of Medicine titled "Heal Your Headache."

\* \* \* \* \* \* \* \* \*

**Getting a Good Night's Sleep**                 **February 2008**

For quite awhile now I've been 'sleeping like a baby.' While we think of this as meaning we're sleeping quite well, that's not really the case—as anyone who's had a baby in the house knows full well. Babies typically sleep fitfully (not sleeping very long at a time), which can make them very irritable. (Note the definition of irritable: easily exasperated or excited, responsive to stimuli.) It's in that sense that I've been sleeping like a baby.

I've tried many of the techniques used to get a baby to sleep—like calming myself down before bed, making sure I'm cozy and warm, keeping the room as dark and quiet as possible, etc. But it's still difficult to sleep for a long period at a time.

None of this is unusual for either babies or older people. Most of us seem to follow a kind of cycle of sleep throughout our lives. First there's the baby stage of sleeping in short bursts, then early childhood when we go to bed early, sleep soundly and wake up very early in the morning. During the teen years there's still a good bit of sound sleeping, but the hours shift dramatically, staying up later at night and sleeping later in the morning—only rousing when forced to do so for school.

Then when we become parents, we adjust our sleeping habits to fit the needs of our children. We become almost like teenagers in that we drag ourselves out of bed earlier than we prefer in order to care for the early-rising youngsters. As our kids become teenagers, we're likely to stay up later than we prefer in order to see that the teens are home safely. By the time the kids are grown, we've adjusted our sleep schedule so many times that it's almost impossible to establish a 'natural' sleep pattern for ourselves. And just as we think we have things under control, we become old enough that we fall into the pattern discussed earlier of 'sleeping like a baby.'

This baby-sleep would be fine in older age—*if* we had no responsibilities and could sleep anytime we wanted. But most of us continue to be quite active and involved in work and other activities so that nap time is not in our schedule. So we try to muddle along, doing the best we can.

All this discussion may seem superficial and unimportant—until we focus on the larger ramifications involved in how we do (or don't) sleep. Sleep has an impact on our energy, our alertness, our stress level, and our overall health—all of which affect almost every aspect of our lives.

We live in such a fast-paced culture that it's getting more and more difficult to get a good night's sleep—or even to just slow down and relax. So the next time you feel tired, rushed, overwhelmed, or generally stressed-out, try getting not just *a* good night's sleep, but *lots* of good nights of sleep. This one change in your lifestyle can make a big difference in being better prepared to handle the challenges we all face throughout our lives.

* * * * * * * * *

**Age is Relative**                                         **June 2006**

Naturally, we all have our very real numerical age—but we also have a sense of what age we feel ourselves to be. And this sense of a particular age can change drastically throughout our lives. For instance, my son turns 42 this week and my daughter was 44 last month.

I find it interesting that having kids in their 40s leads me to feel older than simply being 70 myself. That's partly because we can more easily see the passage of time reflected in our kids than in ourselves. Frankly, it doesn't seem possible that my 'kids' are in their 40s —when it seems like only yesterday that they were small.

While I see both of them as quite young, I recall that I felt I was much older when I was their age. And my own mother felt she was truly old at the age of 40. It seems that each generation feels younger at a given age than those that preceded them—and in general, people today do look and act younger than they used to. In fact, you've probably heard that 50 is the new 30—and other such fantasies. But there's an element of truth to the adage that you're only as old as you feel, especially when you consider the impact of health, fitness, and lifestyle on the way we age.

While we can't change our mathematical age, we do have a lot of control over our aging process. For instance, in most cases, if we take care of ourselves, we can lead a healthy, active life. And on the other side of that coin, we see the significant problems due to the growing crisis of obesity, especially in the U.S. For instance, unfortunately, my mother was significantly overweight most of her life, causing adult onset diabetes that robbed her of her health in every aspect of this disease, including blindness, eventually leading to her death at the age of 71. In many ways watching her loss of health motivated me to try to avoid this fate. So I've worked to maintain a normal weight, and even now at the age of 70 I work out at the YMCA five times a week.

I've also been motivated to reach for what's possible by watching my 98-year-old mother-in-law who still lives alone—albeit with the support of many family members who see her every day. She's truly an inspiration to everyone who knows her. So when I think about age and aging, I tend to see it as being more relative than absolute.

\* \* \* \* \* \* \* \* \*

**The Common Cold—and Cancer**  September 2006

I've always been healthy and had few medical problems—except the time in 1992 when I was diagnosed with breast cancer. And while I know it's a little unusual... I deal much better with the really serious challenges of life (like the cancer) than with the little hassles (like the cold I've had for the past week). In fact, there's something about a summer cold that adds insult to injury and somehow just seems *wrong*.

When I had breast cancer, I felt like I had a little control. I could choose the type of surgery and make determinations about chemo, radiation, tamoxifen, etc. But with a cold, I feel completely powerless. No matter what I do, it doesn't seem to make any difference. In fact, it reminds me of the old saying that 'a cold lasts about seven days if you treat it and about a week if you don't.'

I'm not a patient person. So I kept thinking I could somehow move the process along by getting as much rest as possible—which is a difficult thing for me to do. Of course, I'm also a little stubborn, so when James got the cold first, I decided I would just *refuse* to get it. Of course, I failed on all counts, and I do *not* like feeling helpless and without any control.

Well, I'm better now, none the worse for wear, but this little episode did cause me to stop and wonder how some of the very strong coping skills I bring to bear in crisis situations might be utilized in dealing with these simple hassles of life.

\* \* \* \* \* \* \* \* \*

### Breast Cancer Awareness October 2006

October is breast cancer awareness month. Most women have some awareness of breast cancer, but it's often tinged with an anxiety that can interfere with focusing on it to the extent that would be most beneficial. But if you were to have to face it yourself, you'd find that it's extremely helpful to already be well-informed.

In 1992, I was diagnosed with breast cancer—and since my mother and grandmother had both had breast cancer, I'd considered it my responsibility to make sure I was informed. And I'm so glad I was. *After* you're diagnosed is no time to begin the process of learning about breast cancer—and

## Health and Fitness

particularly about the various options and decisions you must make.

Your doctor may make certain recommendations, but each woman determines for herself her precise plan of treatment, beginning with deciding whether to have a lumpectomy or a mastectomy—which, by the way, are shown to be equally effective unless the tumor is larger.

I feel fortunate that it has now been 14 years since my cancer—and I have not had a recurrence. Since my lump was 2.5 cm with lymph node involvement, I had Stage II cancer, which statistically meant I had a 65% chance of 5-year survival. (With the treatments I underwent, that statistic moved up to 75% chance of 5-year survival.) But I have not spent these years worrying about my prospects, despite knowing that there are no guarantees about the future—no matter how many years have passed.

I have, however, done a variety of things to support breast cancer awareness and recovery. Back when I was going through surgery, chemo, and radiation, I made three television appearances at three-month intervals, each time discussing the particular stage I was going through—including changing wigs on camera to demonstrate different wig possibilities. (Believe me, that was a real TV moment!)

And I conducted a seminar for breast cancer survivors where everyone went beyond focusing on the obvious downsides of this experience to share whatever positive things they might have gained as well. Many people shared wonderful stories of how it was a wake-up call to better appreciate life and the people they love. I also wrote an article for a Health Clinic's newsletter, addressing this whole issue.

But most of my efforts were undertaken during the first few years after my own cancer. I felt it was time to move away from too intense a focus on the cancer because I didn't feel it *defined* me as a person and I didn't want to filter my identity through being a 'cancer survivor.'

But this year, due to wanting to support a friend who is undergoing breast cancer treatment, I'm going to participate in a cancer awareness event—one of many that are held across the U.S. It's the annual Race for the Cure sponsored by the Susan G. Komen Breast Cancer Foundation.

I also fulfilled my personal responsibility by getting my annual mammogram last week—which I encourage every woman over 40 to do. The whole idea of focusing on breast cancer may bother some people, but trying to ignore it doesn't do anything to protect you (or someone you love). So I hope everyone will make it their business to become more aware and better informed about this important health issue.

\* \* \* \* \* \* \* \* \*

**Living with Breast Cancer**                      **March 2007**

The recent announcement of a recurrence of Elizabeth Edwards' breast cancer has pushed this issue into the public spotlight in a significant way. Of course, this issue is already significant to many of us who have been diagnosed with breast cancer.

It was 15 years ago this month that I received my diagnosis and underwent the same treatment as Elizabeth Edwards: lumpectomy, radiation and chemo. I feel extremely fortunate that I've had no recurrence in all these years, but I always recognized the possibility. I was fortunate not only to have read "Dr. Susan Love's Breast Book," but to have heard her speak in person. She made it clear that microscopic cancer cells remain in the body and can create problems down the road.

In fact, I observed this happening a few years ago when a friend had a recurrence of the breast cancer she had first experienced about the same time as mine. We'd shared our experiences and formed a special bond, so I was especially saddened when she later died from a recurrence of the cancer.

I respect each person's decision as to how to handle this. I admired my friend who kept her recurrence private, and I also admire Elizabeth who is speaking out publicly. In fact, I expect Elizabeth's candor will play an important role in raising awareness and understanding about all aspects of dealing with cancer—much the way Betty Ford first did back in 1974 when she went public about her breast cancer.

I've found it inspiring to watch Elizabeth Edwards talk about the way she's facing this new crisis in her life, and I find myself with some strong emotions about the recurrence of her cancer. I think that's because a recurrence is a far more critical situation than an initial diagnosis. Medical treatments are constantly improving, but still have a long way to go. So it will be with much personal interest and concern that I continue to follow her story.

Of course, paying attention to breast cancer has been a lifelong practice for me since it 'runs in the family.' And since I have a daughter and three granddaughters, I anticipate this being an issue of special interest for the rest of my life. I do hope that out of this current public attention to the disease, many more people will become better informed and prepared to do what they can to avoid it or to more effectively deal with it if it happens to them or to someone they love.

* * * * * * * *

## Minor Surgery    June 2006

I assume that whoever came up with the distinction between minor surgery and major surgery was trying to distinguish between whether or not it was life-threatening. This is a legitimate distinction—and one that I personally recognize since I've witnessed both. But *any* surgery creates a degree of uncertainty and vulnerability that takes us away from our day-to-day way of being in the world.

This week James had hernia surgery. Due to scar tissue from a previous surgery, they couldn't use the laparoscopic method, so they made a small incision, inserted mesh, etc. Anyway, everything went well and his progress the past few days has been normal. (Normal, that is, for post-surgery—but, of course, not really normal.)

Since we like to have as much understanding as possible about the details surrounding any medical procedure and recovery, we spent a lot of time trying to get good information about all aspects of this whole experience. It didn't help that the doctor, who had said he would follow up the next day, failed to do so. But it was clear that everything was going as it *should*, so we weren't actually worried, just curious.

Anyway, the main point I want to focus on is the way we found a certain positive quality to the different tone of these days of recovery. Naturally, he wasn't able to proceed with his normal routine. (Although as anyone who has had any kind of surgery knows, he did a good bit of walking after the first day—which is the recommended way of speeding recovery.) And since I'm the ultimate nurturer, I abandoned many of my daily responsibilities, instead focusing on him and his needs—including just lying on the bed talking to help him pass the time.

*Health and Fitness*

We found the slower pace quite refreshing, another reminder of how much we rush ourselves and hassle ourselves over so many details in life that don't warrant the degree of attention we give them. In fact, I think that this recovery period provided a kind of guilt-free cover for relaxing in a way we seldom allow ourselves. Not only did we enjoy the slower pace of the day, but simply sitting on the patio watching the rabbits (which we always enjoy) was even more enjoyable.

The whole world seemed to slow down. It was as if since the body couldn't be rushed, nothing else would be rushed either. We even ate our food more slowly and found more awareness and enjoyment of the tastes. So while I don't recommend anyone having surgery or any other medical procedure unless it's absolutely necessary, it's interesting to note that we can find some good in almost any life experience.

\* \* \* \* \* \* \* \* \*

## What You Don't Know *Can* Hurt You        July 2007

The debate about how to address the problems with the healthcare system in the U.S. has been going on for years. It's so complex that I've never been able to develop an 'informed opinion' about it. (This is unusual for me, since I usually have an opinion about everything.)

However, I've recently become much more informed, and I want to share some of what I learned. One source of information was an article by economist Paul Krugman. Below is an excerpt:

> *"Every wealthy country except the United States already has some form of universal care. Citizens of these countries pay extra taxes as a result—but they make up for*

that through savings on insurance premiums and out-of-pocket medical costs. The overall cost of health care in countries with universal coverage is much lower than it is here.

"Meanwhile, every available indicator says that in terms of quality, access to needed care and health outcomes, the U.S. health care system does worse, not better, than other advanced countries—even Britain, which spends only about 40 percent as much per person as we do."

Another source of information is the movie "Sicko." (The fact that it's a Michael Moore movie does *not* mean it can be dismissed as partisan rhetoric. In fact, many of his strongest critics in the Republican party have endorsed the film.)

Moore is quoted as saying:

"I made this film in hopes of reaching across the great divide in this country, so I made it in a non-partisan way. I started with the premise that illness knows no political stripe. I've had Republicans come up to me after a screening and shake my hand and thank me."

A more objective assessment of the movie is reflected by the results of a CNN report that 'fact-checked' the movie. Here's what they reported:

—From the Centers for Disease Control and Prevention:
43.6 million, or about 15 percent of Americans, were uninsured in 2006.

—According to the Institute of Medicine:
18,000 people die each year due to being uninsured.

—Also from the Institute of Medicine:
The U.S. spends more of its gross domestic product on health care than any other country. (The United States

## Health and Fitness

spends more than 15 percent of its GDP on health care. No other nation even comes close to that number. France spends about 11 percent, and Canadians spend 10 percent.)

—According to the World Health Organization:
Both the French and Canadian systems rank in the Top 10 of the world's best health-care systems. The United States comes in at No. 37 (just slightly ahead of Slovenia).

Broader perspective provided by the movie:
It was striking to see that health care in some countries (like France and Canada) is entirely free to every citizen—and that people in those countries had a hard time comprehending how U.S. citizens must buy insurance or pay for their own health care.

Other democratic countries with universal health care believe it's their democracy (and the power of the people in being unwilling to tolerate anything less) that allows them to have universal health care. A key part of their position is the fact that they think in terms of *we*, while in the U.S. we generally think in terms of *me*.

While working toward universal coverage for everyone is 'the right thing to do,' there's also a very strong reason to make this effort in our own self-interest. That's because it would be a mistake to assume that as long as you have good health insurance, then none of this affects you personally.

Why you need to see this film:
The primary point of the movie (and the most shocking aspect) was the mistreatment of those who *do* have insurance. One of the most riveting scenes involved testimony from a woman who'd worked within the 'medical-industrial complex,' confessing her role in systematically denying payment for

medical procedures based solely on efforts to save money for the company.

The movie makes it clear that many of the policies create a medical and financial nightmare from which no one is immune. This situation is a threat to all those who think they can count on their insurance when they need it—and exposes the fact that 'what you don't know *can* hurt you.' (In fact, it just might kill you.)

So everyone needs to be better informed and more active in supporting efforts to reform our health-care system.

\* \* \* \* \* \* \* \* \*

### Modern Medical Advances                    January 2008

This past week I was witness to some modern medical advances—when two people close to me underwent surgical procedures. While I have some concerns about many aspects of medical care today, the advances in surgical techniques are quite impressive. For instance, I've seen the differences over the years in the approaches to surgery for breast cancer. My mother had surgery 30 years ago, I had it 16 years ago, and a close family member had it just last week.

Back 30 years ago, there was no consideration of any treatment other than a radical mastectomy. Since my mother was a very large woman and the surgery was extensive, her recovery was slow and difficult. Then 16 years ago, my breast surgery entailed having a lumpectomy—with a much easier recovery time from the surgery itself. Of course, the overall recovery time was quite long and challenging, involving both chemo and radiation. Now breast cancer surgery is done with

## Health and Fitness

minimal invasion and minimal pain, even allowing the patient to go home the day of surgery if they choose.

A much more dramatic illustration of the changes in modern medicine can be seen in the treatments for heart problems. It was 36 years ago that my father developed some symptoms of heart problems, but an EKG showed nothing. The following day, he began having intensive heart pain and walked the one block from his work to the doctor's office. He had a major heart attack there in the doctor's office and died while the doctor looked on, unable to take steps to save him.

However, just three years ago when my son began having symptoms of heart problems, he went to the emergency room where they determined he was having a heart attack. They immediately put him on medication to 'suspend' the attack while they airlifted him to a hospital equipped to do angioplasty surgery to open up the blocked artery and insert a stent. The operation was successful—and he walked out of the hospital the next day.

Another area of great advances in modern medicine is the use of arthroscopic surgery. When my husband had arthroscopic knee surgery, it was done as an outpatient, requiring a stay of only three hours. And without the need for crutches, he walked from the car to the house. The additional treatment involved the basics like icing the knee, elevating the leg, etc., but did not involve pain.

While advances in surgical treatments are mostly positive, the increase in the use of prescription medications can be quite a different matter. We've generally become far too dependent on the advertisements by pharmaceutical companies to drive our increased reliance on drugs to take care of whatever ails us. It's important to consider that any drug strong enough to have a positive impact is also strong enough to have a significant negative impact, particularly when combined with a number of other drugs.

Unfortunately, many people (especially as they get older) come to rely on drugs—and just *assume* this is necessary in order to continue to function. My husband and I have had multiple experiences where medical or insurance people are quite surprised that we take no prescription drugs. It's become such a way of life that it's almost *expected* that all older people are taking several medications.

We recognize that we're fortunate to still have good health in our early 70s, but we also know that we work hard to maintain it. We're constantly trying to determine what we can do for ourselves in sustaining our health in order to avoid having to rely on drugs to do it for us. We recognize that failing to eat a healthy diet and failing to get regular exercise are at the heart of much of the need for drugs taken on an ongoing basis.

It's great to have drugs when truly needed and when there's no good alternative, but taking them as a routine matter is highly questionable. And taking multiple drugs serves to set up a cycle of taking even more drugs. That's because each new drug causes side effects that need to be offset by still another drug. When taking many different drugs, it's impossible to fully determine all the drug interactions in general—and it's impossible to determine the interactions for a specific person.

So 'modern medical advances' are advances only if we use them wisely. Just because more options are available doesn't mean it's best to depend on them—unless and until there are no other options. It's important for everyone (of any age) to think long term about how to keep your body in condition to serve you well for many healthy years in the future.

*Health and Fitness*

\* \* \* \* \* \* \* \* \*

**Losing my Mind**                                          **June 2007**

When I walk into a room to get something and can't remember what it was, I have a momentary feeling of foolishness. When I can't recall the name of some well-known person or can't remember where I put something, I have another of those disorienting moments.

Most of us have these moments of forgetfulness throughout out lives, and we don't think much about them. But when you start getting a little older (and when there's a lot of media attention on Alzheimer's, as has happened lately), it gives you a little more pause than usual.

In fact, it's beginning to look like Alzheimer's is going to be a much greater problem in the coming years, as more people live longer. The numbers make it clear that it will touch every family in some way—either as a person who has the disease or as a caregiver. For instance, I read one report saying that 50% of those over age 85 will develop Alzheimer's.

According to a report in Psychology Today magazine:

*"In 2020, there will be a 27 percent increase in cases compared with today's numbers, and by 2030 rates will climb 70 percent. And by 2050, unless science intervenes, cases will rise nearly 300 percent, or 13.2 million people. Currently, an estimated 4.5 million Americans have Alzheimer's."*

The work with genes may allow people to find out whether they have inherited a predisposition for the disease. In the meantime, we can look to our own ancestors for some clues. When I apply this in my own family, I find reason to be hopeful. My mother died at age 71 (the age I am now), so I have no indication about her, but my two grandmothers lived until ages 89 and 95 and both of them were very sharp until the end. My husband's prospects also look hopeful based on his family history. In fact, his mother is now 99 years old, and she's 100% lucid and as mentally alert as ever.

However, for everyone (regardless of family history) there is hope based on the anticipation that within a few years there will be treatments that may be able to stop the progression of the disease and perhaps even somewhat reverse it.

The reason to focus on this issue now is not to create undue concern or fear of the future, but to point out what we can do to help ourselves—regardless of genetics or medications. As with so many other diseases, it helps if we take steps to stay physically and mentally active. We've all heard the old saying, "use it or lose it." So I'm committing to fitness and to learning on a continuous basis for the rest of my life—in hopes of avoiding 'losing my mind.'

## Chapter 10: Learning/Education

School Days
How's Your Education?
Public Education
Graduation Day
Lifelong Learning
Bookaholics
Awards that Matter

*Learning/Education*

**School Days**  August 2007

During these waning days of summer, thoughts turn to going back to school. While I've always had a special interest in education, it's particularly heightened due to the increasing problems faced by schools these days. Everyone is affected: teachers, students, parents, grandparents, etc.

I have three grandchildren, and this year they'll be in three different schools; one is in elementary school, one is in middle school and one is in high school. In addition to anticipating the classes and activities of the three schools, there's also the practical factor of providing transportation for three different locations.

But rather than discussing the particular issues related to the upcoming school year for our family, I want to invite everyone to focus on our education system as a whole—whether or not you have a family member currently in school. (After all, everyone's taxes pay for our education system.)

There's a tendency for each generation to hold a (revised?) memory of their own school days, so I acknowledge that's probably the case with me. However, I do know that my school situation was far simpler than the one that exists today.

For instance, I lived in the same small town for the 12 years of my public education, attending only two schools. (There was one school for 1st through 6th grades, and another school for 7th through 12th grades.) I had almost all the same classmates for all 12 years, including the 'boy' who has now been my husband for over 50 years. And, quite significantly, the teachers were community members that I knew outside the school scene.

Even though this was a small town in the deep south in the 40s and 50s, I look back now with amazement at the quality of the education I received. For instance, my husband and I both found we were fully qualified to succeed, even excel, in our pursuit of higher education. And perhaps more significantly, we developed a lifelong love of learning.

One of my concerns about today's education system is that the focus on discipline, testing, crumbling physical structures, etc., is systematically killing the potential for developing an attitude toward learning that will continue throughout students' lives. This is not just a serious problem for today's students; it's a problem for everyone who fully appreciates that it's not just a cliché that 'The children are our future.'

We only have to pay attention to the news to see that many of the most successful entrepreneurs today (responsible for some of the most important changes taking place in the world) are young people who are barely out of school, if not still in school. So it behooves each of us to accept a certain personal responsibility for speaking up and taking action in any way that makes sense in our own communities.

Of course, it's also important to recognize that we can't be concerned *only* about our own communities; we must also care about what happens to *all* communities. In the global society in which we live today, "no man/woman/child is an island." What happens to 'the least of these' affects all of us.

\* \* \* \* \* \* \* \*

### How's Your Education?   September 2006

It's back-to-school time again—a yearly ritual filled with excitement mixed with a little trepidation. There are a few differences this year in that there are a lot of news reports about

*Learning/Education*

the negative impact of homework on students—and on their families.

For instance, last week Time Magazine had a full-page commentary about homework, highlighting the information in two new books: "The Homework Myth" by Alfie Kohn and "The Case Against Homework" by Sara Bennett and Nancy Kalish. Both books make the case that homework is 'oppressing families and making kids hate learning.'

Then this week's cover of Newsweek Magazine continues the theme, with an article focusing on "The New First Grade: Too Much Too Soon?" It's not as if all this homework is making our kids perform better—or learn more. In fact, it's just the opposite.

Despite the amount of time spent on homework increasing 51% since 1981, an exhaustive review by the nation's top homework scholar, Duke University's Harris Cooper, concluded that homework does not measurably improve academic achievement for kids in grade school.

While 'testing' also gets a lot of attention (and also shows a lack of actual improvement in learning), homework has long been my number one area of concern about school. Actually, I don't remember having any homework issues when I was in school, completing whatever homework was assigned during library/study hall.

However, things had changed dramatically by the time my own kids were in school. I still vividly recall the negative impact of homework on our home life. In fact, I remember one teacher's disbelief when my response to her asking me to insist that my kids spend more time on homework was that I didn't believe a lot of homework was a good idea and I would not support it.

Since today's homework is far more challenging, I'm concerned all over again for the impact on my three grandchildren—and on their home life. And when combined with the huge increase in after-school activities, most families have almost no quality time together at home.

Let me quickly add that I strongly believe in *learning* (including 'lifelong learning'), but I'm concerned that today's formal education is more about studying for tests than about learning.

In fact, in today's world where so much information is available at your fingertips through the Internet, a strong case can be made for placing much less emphasis on memorizing facts and much more attention on the processes of thinking, organizing, problem-solving, recognizing patterns, and finding meaning and significance.

In other words, in such a fast-moving world, we need to focus less on learning facts and more on 'learning how to learn.'

For many years I've saved an anonymous quote titled "On School."

—*Very little of what is taught in school is learned.*
—*Very little of what is learned is remembered.*
—*Very little of what is remembered is used.*

But I don't think it has to be that way. In fact, here are the words to a little song I wrote about 30 years ago and sang for the teachers of my kids' school at that time. I called it "How's Your Education."

*How's your education?*
*Have you learned your ABC's?*
*Learned your reading, writing and arithmetic*
*and all those things that please?*

*Learning/Education*

*Well that's a good beginning
for the left side of your brain,
but there's another side to learning
And that's the one I want to explain.*

*You see the left side works by reason
and rationality,
and it does all the talking
for everyone, both you and me.*

*But the right side is important
though it never says a word.
You see it's silent and observant
with a still, small voice that's never heard.*

*So we tend to forget it
no matter how it tries.
We use the 3 R's of our left side
and forget the right's 3 I's.*

*The first is Intuition,
then Ingenuity,
and then Imagination
to be the best that we can be.*

*So if we want a lot of learning
we'll use both sides of our brain,
and we'll plan our education
so that both of them we train.*

\* \* \* \* \* \* \* \* \*

**Public Education** August 2006

Education is highly valued in countries with limited (or nonexistent) educational opportunities. And while the U.S. offers free public education for all, it fails to fulfill the promise of providing a *quality* education for every child. Naturally, there are some excellent public schools, but there are far too many others that fail in fundamental ways. For instance, 20 years ago, the U.S. was #1 in key subjects like math, but today we don't even make the top 20.

This has not gone unnoticed by our government, as well as by others who are dedicated to finding ways to address this decline. The Bill and Melinda Gates Foundation is spearheading one of the largest efforts, but many other dedicated individuals are coming up with creative ways to change the way some schools function. Despite these pockets of successful efforts, the number of kids who 'fall through the cracks' continues to grow.

My three grandchildren are in public school, and they're fortunate to live in an area with good quality schools and resources. But we need to have compassion for those who are *not* so fortunate—and also to appreciate how the lack of education for all kids directly affects all of us in many significant ways.

For instance, 80% of the prisoners in American jails and prisons are high school dropouts. And 600,000 of these people are released from jail each year, unprepared to succeed in life without an education—thus perpetuating a lifestyle of poverty and crime that affects everyone.

In addition to the human price for the failure of our schools is the financial price. For instance, in California where I live, we spend approximately $10,000 per year per student, but we

*Learning/Education*

spend $34,000 per year per prisoner. Due to the high percentage of prisoners who are not prepared to successfully function in society when they're released, this is a sobering comment on the prospects for the future regarding both crime and education.

While money alone won't solve the problems in our public school system, it's an essential starting point for any effort to make education equally available to all kids. In fact, any effort that allows *some* kids to get a better education while at the same time leaving others in poorly equipped schools with poorly-paid teachers simply perpetuates the failure of the system as a whole—and the resulting negative impact on society as a whole.

So the basic question is how to bring more equality of opportunity to all children. And it seems to me that it starts with ensuring that an equal amount of resources (money, buildings, teachers, extras) are dedicated to each student. But how can this be accomplished within our nationwide school system when each state and each school board is responsible for making decisions and distributing resources?

Many smart people have thought about this question for a long time, so I don't expect to come up with any ideas that haven't already been considered. But I keep coming back to the need to find a way to equally distribute the money that pays for the buildings, the equipment, the teachers, etc.

As I mentioned above, for instance, California spends about $10,000 per student. (A different source indicates that the spending per student is $7,500.) But whatever the precise amount, you can be sure that the number is reached by mathematically dividing the total amount spent on public education by the number of students—and does *not* reflect an amount spent equally on each individual student. Some schools receive far more per student and others considerably less.

For instance, some schools have sparkling buildings with extra features, small class sizes, and money to hire the best teachers—while others have leaking buildings with broken windows, too few desks or supplies, no extras, overcrowded class sizes, and no money to hire well-qualified teachers.

Unfortunately, we're not likely to make any significant difference in the problem with public schools unless and until funds are actually distributed equally per student, allowing all schools to have the kind of resources that can make a difference.

It's not enough for each of us to only focus on 'me and mine.' Focusing only on the alternatives available to each of us personally (like the ability to live in a nicer area of town, pay for a private school or get a school voucher) leaves those who are *not* able to do these things even worse off than before. And based on the correlation between school dropouts and the large numbers of young adults in prison, the problems with our public education system actually make *all* of us worse off.

Some people may resist the idea of having some of their local taxes that are earmarked for education go to kids outside their particular school district. However, people who have no children at all pay taxes that go towards education, so already we don't pay taxes *only* for 'our children.' So if California (and every other state) actually allocated education monies based on an equal amount per student, it could be the first step to addressing not only the problem with public education, but the human problem for those who fail to receive an education—and the impact of their failure on all of us.

\* \* \* \* \* \* \* \* \*

*Learning/Education*

**Graduation Day**  May 2007

Graduation is a special day in the lives of young people. And I'm looking forward to the upcoming graduations of two of my grandchildren—one from elementary school and one from middle school. Even though we don't consider these the *major* graduations of our lives, each one marks a special point in our educational life and is a time of celebration for the graduates and their families.

One of the most celebratory graduations in our family was when our daughter graduated Magna Cum Laude from law school when she was three months pregnant with her first child. Our group at the ceremony included her husband, his parents, her brother, her grandmother, and us, her parents. We all thoroughly enjoyed the event, even releasing a huge bunch of balloons at the moment she was handed her diploma.

No matter what the nature of a particular graduation, most people remember their own quite vividly—and fondly. And almost everyone has a graduation story to tell. In fact, I have several stories I'd like to share.

My high school graduation was relatively uneventful for me personally, but there were a couple of special things associated with it. First was my graduation dress—because it was the first 'ready-made' dress I'd ever owned. Since we had very little money growing up, my mother made all my clothes. This was *not* a hardship because she was an extraordinary seamstress, so much so that I was voted 'best dressed' in high school.

The other noteworthy aspect to high school graduation was that James (my steady boyfriend at the time and my husband for the past 50+ years) skipped graduation in order to travel to the site of the finals of the state high school tennis championships to be played the following day. He was thrilled to be in the finals and wanted to be sure he was prepared to play his best. Understandably, although they allowed it, his family did not appreciate his decision.

Since we were married while attending college (and I was working full-time and taking a few courses), I didn't graduate until many years later. But James' college graduation was an especially important event for his mother, since she had not been able to celebrate his high school graduation. In fact, even though it involved a good bit of traveling, she managed to attend each of his graduations as he went on to get an M.A. and a Ph.D.

My own completion of college (and graduation) happened many years later—because once James began working full-time, I wanted to have kids and stay home with them while they were young. So it wasn't until 1979 (at the age of 43, with kids ages 17 and 15), that I finally graduated from college.

My graduation at 43 was nothing compared to a story in the news recently about a woman of 95 graduating from college along with her granddaughter. And she's not slowing down now; she plans to get a job on a cruise ship as a storyteller.

One reason my college experience was so special is that Antioch in Yellow Springs, Ohio, was a very unusual college. Student representatives played an active role in establishing the policies of the school, the school's evaluation system didn't necessarily involve grades, and the percentage of graduates who went on to graduate schools was the second highest in the U.S., just behind Harvard at the time. But perhaps the most distinctive difference was in its graduation—which was a very unique experience. It was held outside with all the graduates dressed however they pleased. It was a totally joyful celebration.

Frankly, it's not any particular graduation itself that's significant; it's the learning that it represents. But learning is certainly not restricted to (or necessarily best accomplished through) formal education. If our formal education systems really do their jobs, they'll prepare us for a lifetime of learning. So it's important to not only enjoy the graduations in your life, but to appreciate the importance of lifelong learning.

* * * * * * * * *

**Lifelong Learning**                                        **April 2007**

This is Spring Break week for lots of schools, including the ones my grandchildren attend. Naturally, they enjoy this break from their regular routine, but fortunately, they are all in good schools and generally are thriving in their learning experience.

It's important that children get a sense of the enjoyment of the learning process—because our formal education is only the beginning of what should be 'lifelong learning.' There's much more to learn than can be taught in school. In fact, what you know today is going to be outdated tomorrow, so it's not 'what you know' that's most important, it's 'how you learn.' The overwhelming goal needs to be 'learning how to learn!'

Learning really is a lifelong process. In fact, this ongoing learning relates to the way the brain undergoes significant neurological changes at different ages and stages of life, providing special 'windows of opportunity' for certain kinds of learning.

It begins before we're born when the early stages of the brain are developing. Then during the first year of life, a child's brain is being 'wired,' providing the foundation that allows them to maximize later brain developments. Based on neurological studies done in the 80s, there are additional important brain developments at around ages 7, 11, and 15—with full brain development not completed until age 21.

But that certainly doesn't mean that we quit learning and building 'connections.' In fact, the most important work of the brain can only be done by continuing the process that *begins* with a fully-developed brain. For instance, what we learn is only the raw 'information,' made up of facts and ideas. Then the information is organized in such a way as to allow for 'knowledge.' Finally, this knowledge is integrated into a whole that is more useful than the sum of its parts, allowing for 'wisdom.'

This kind of wisdom can also arise as a by-product of age—*if* the years have been spent continuing to learn. I'm personally pleased that older generations like my own are prepared to contribute to the learning process by passing down their insight, experience and wisdom to future generations.

As evidence of this ability for lifelong learning, I'd like to close with an excerpt from a Wall Street Journal article (February 17, 2007) by Sharon Begley, "Parts of brain seem to get better with age."

> *"An emerging body of research shows that a surprising array of mental functions hold up well into old age, while others actually get better. Vocabulary improves, as do other verbal abilities such as facility with synonyms and antonyms. Older brains are packed with more 'expert knowledge'— information relevant to your occupation or hobby. They also store more 'cognitive templates,' or mental outlines of generic problems and solutions that can be tapped when confronting new problems."*

*Learning/Education*

It's good to know that everyone is capable of continuing to learn throughout their lives, so I hope you'll make a point to read and think and talk about a wide variety of issues, taking advantage of the rewards of lifelong learning.

\* \* \* \* \* \* \* \* \*

**Bookaholics**                                                   **January 2007**

As James and I accumulated more and more books through the years, we began referring to ourselves as 'bookaholics.' Frankly, I thought we made up the word, but I find in searching Google that it's quite widely used these days.

For those of you who aren't quite clear about what's involved in being a bookaholic... the best way to describe it is by sharing the words of a couple of bookaholics who lived many years ago.

Thomas Jefferson said, *"I cannot live without books."*

Erasmus said, *"When I get a little money, I buy books; And if any is left, I buy food and clothes."*

For a long time we accumulated books (reading *almost* all of them), until our library reached into the thousands. James built a couple of wall-sized bookcases that could be moved as we relocated. However, with each successive move to smaller and smaller living spaces, we've gradually sorted through the books, giving away the ones we could bear to part with.

Now we're in a paring-down process that requires us to part with *most* of the books, keeping only those we anticipate repeatedly re-reading in future years.

I must say, however, that I'm finding this sorting process to be less difficult than I anticipated. I realize that each book meant a lot to me when I first read it, but I don't need to re-read most of them because I 'got the message' the first time.

I should clarify that we only have four or five fiction books, and I won't be keeping any of them. I've always found nonfiction to be far more interesting and exciting than any story that can be made up. I realize this sounds strange, given all the great literature that exists, but it's just my personal preference.

Anyway, I'm thoroughly enjoying going through the books to choose those few to hold on to for re-reading. Almost all of my favorites are quite old and may no longer be available, making them all the more special to me.

For the sake of those of you who are also bookaholics and may want to check them out... Here's a list (alphabetical by author) of a dozen books I've chosen as my favorites. (I also have a number of physics books among my favorites, but my oldest granddaughter shares my interest, so I'm giving those special books to her.)

    Carlson, Richard—Don't Sweat the Small Stuff
    Frankl, Viktor—Man's Search for Meaning
    Kramer, Joel—The Passionate Mind
    Lindbergh, Anne Morrow—Gift from the Sea
    Rosenthal, Ted—How Could I Not Be Among You?
    Ruiz, Don Miguel—The Four Agreements Companion Book
    Salk, Jonas—The Survival of the Wisest
    Sarton, May—Journal of a Solitude
    Shah, Idries—The Sufis
    Teilhard de Chardin—The Phenomenon of Man
    Watts, Alan W.—The Wisdom of Insecurity
    Wheelis, Allen—On Not Knowing How to Live

*Learning/Education*

Footnote: Richard Carlson, author of the first book on the list ("Don't Sweat the Small Stuff") died of a cardiac arrest at the age of 45 in December 2006. This is another reminder of the importance of living our lives in as conscious a way as possible, not waiting for some future time when things will be different.

\* \* \* \* \* \* \* \* \*

**Awards that Matter**                                        **March 2008**

We're coming to the end of what has been called 'awards season'—the time of year when you can hardly turn on TV without encountering an Awards Show of some kind. In fact, there are so many of them that many people have 'tuned out,' deeming them to be less significant than in the past.

However, I recently witnessed an Awards Ceremony that was extremely significant and meaningful. It was held in the Public Middle School attended by one of my grandchildren. While there are many serious problems with providing quality public education today, this was an example of public education at its best.

At the end of each semester a ceremony is held for each grade, honoring all those students who received a 4.0 in Citizenship or Scholarship (or both) during the previous semester. All the students are seated on the stage during the entire program, and as each name is called they come down front to receive their certificate. When the front of the stage is filled, there is enthusiastic applause by friends and family and much photo-taking. The children beam with pride and return to their seats.

This is precisely the kind of recognition that brings out the best in students and reinforces the value of their efforts. And best of all, it reinforces the importance of succeeding not only academically, but also as a good citizen. The same importance is placed on the quality of their character as on their academic accomplishments. This recognition sends a clear message that being a good person and doing well academically are both valuable aspects of a well-rounded student.

It's tempting to focus only on the problems with our school system or with our young people, but we also need to devote more attention to focusing on their successes. While it's great for young people to receive this kind of public recognition, it's also critical that they be recognized within their own families for their successes—as well as for any positive efforts they make to improve themselves in any way.

No child is born 'bad' or born 'a failure.' Their potential is dictated by how we (as individuals and as a society) condition them to think about themselves and their possibilities. There are many instances where young people have overcome incredible odds to make something of themselves. And with more effort on the part of all of us in supporting them, the numbers will continue to grow.

While the effort to identify and support the best in our young people is the *right* thing to do, it's also the *smart* thing to do. Any country or culture that fails to utilize the strengths of its young people will find itself losing out to other countries or cultures that do offer this kind of support. Of course, in a broader context, the kind of global society we all now inhabit means it's not enough only to think of 'us and ours.' We need to rise to the challenge of supporting *all* young people in developing their capacity to make the future a better place for everyone.

# Chapter 11: Technology

Me and My Computer
Internet Savvy
Love/Hate Relationship

*Technology*

## Me and My Computer            March 2007

Our computers allow us to more efficiently manage a wide range of activities that are important in our lives. I especially appreciate this because I remember the days when the standard mode of writing was on a typewriter. In fact, one of my first jobs was as a legal secretary where I had to type an original and six carbon copies of legal documents. (Believe me, that was a challenge and a very tense experience.)

Of course, that was many years ago, but even in 1980 when we wrote our first book, I was still having to use a cut-and-paste process in the course of writing and editing the book. With the speed of modern computers, it's hard to imagine anything that time-consuming today. In fact, we tend to get addicted to the speed of the computer and want faster and faster processors or programs. It's easy to become impatient with waiting a few seconds for a program to launch or a page on the Internet to load.

Anyway, I now have a brand new laptop computer, but it wasn't so much because I wanted more speed as that I was concerned about the age of my old processor. A few strange quirks in the old processor made me nervous about losing some of my data. Even though I'm good about regularly backing up, it was still a major concern—and I feel much better now that I have a new computer.

You see, the great thing about this new laptop is that I get 'two for one' in this machine. We'd been wanting a good laptop anyway, so I'm using it both as a laptop—*and* as my processor. I have my monitor, keyboard and mouse hooked up to the laptop, which works perfectly. There's even a little remote control so I don't have to open the laptop to start my computer. And, of course, another advantage to this arrangement is that now whenever I travel, all my data, including all my email records, etc., are already on my laptop.

My only hesitancy in making this move was some concern about my programs and data being successfully transferred to the new laptop. But all went well, thanks to my son—who, fortunately, happens to be an IT professional. Without his expertise, this transfer would have been impossible for me. I'm a very pleased to have this new, safer computer to support me in my daily work.

\* \* \* \* \* \* \* \* \*

### Internet Savvy                                           July 2007

I've had my website for eleven years and have been using the Internet longer than that, but I'm still baffled as to just how it all works. I even bought a big, glossy book titled "How the Internet Works" by Preston Gralla that contains an enormous amount of information (including beautiful illustrations and diagrams), but I still have difficulty *really* understanding much of the actual workings of the Internet.

Of course, I realize I'm not alone; most of us are not technically savvy about the Internet. However, it's critical that all of us are well-informed about how to *use* the Internet, particularly when it comes to maintaining our safety and privacy. This has become an even greater concern for me personally now that my oldest granddaughter has begun using the Internet more extensively, as well as recently getting her own email account.

It's important to know how to protect yourself—whether you're an adult or a child. Here are a couple of general rules that can help:

## Technology

—Don't click on a 'pop-up' ad (or any other kind of pop-up) on a website.

—Don't open an email attachment unless it's from someone you personally know and trust.

Another issue with email is that it's almost impossible to avoid receiving 'junk mail' of an unsavory nature. This is a problem for adults as well as kids; and even with software designed to block most of it, some always gets through. Also, with porn sites being so prevalent on the Internet, any 'search' is likely to bring up pages that are not appropriate for kids.

Fortunately, my daughter is very diligent about monitoring my granddaughter's use of the Internet, and I'm talking to her about it as well. I recently passed on to her an article about the risks in posting any personal information online. Internet sites like MySpace are particularly popular among teenagers and can be one of the many tools kids use to stay in touch with each other. But there are downsides to this kind of public posting as well.

This risk is well-illustrated by the TV series about child predators who are caught coming to see young kids they met through the Internet. But there are many less obvious risks that may take awhile to come to fruition. For instance, many years later, colleges or future employers may find information about you that prevents you from getting the job you want or getting into the college you prefer.

It's not just your words that need to be guarded; it's also photos and videos that can create future problems from unwanted exposure.

Here are some other general rules that can be helpful:

—Don't share any embarrassing personal photos that others might upload to the Web.

—Don't participate in any embarrassing videos that could find their way onto YouTube.

One thing many people (perhaps especially young people) don't fully appreciate about the Internet is that once it's 'out there,' it's never really 'gone'—even if you *think* you've deleted it. In other words, once the Genie is out of the bottle, there's no putting it back.

Having said all this, the Internet is here to stay, so there's no point in trying to avoid it or to bemoan the problems associated with it. The key is to be as informed as possible and as diligent as possible in how you use it. For instance, it's wise to avoid any personal, individual contact with strangers. That includes avoiding private chat rooms and personal emails with strangers, as well as not sharing personal information as to your real identity or location.

The bottom line is that you need to be as judicious as possible in how you use the Internet, protecting yourself while benefiting from what it has to offer. As for me personally, I intend to continue to be an active member of the Internet community and to take advantage of the access to vital information that is made possible through this marvel of technology.

\* \* \* \* \* \* \* \* \*

## Love/Hate Relationship          April 2008

Most of us have a love/hate relationship with our computers. (It's like the old saying, 'Can't live with them and can't live without them.') I'm more focused on computer issues right now because I'm involved in a big project that includes launching an additional website, adding to my shopping cart, etc., all of which is made more complicated by the fact that I have a new operating system and many of my old software programs 'don't play nicely' (aren't compatible) with the new system.

I realize it's not fair to blame the computer itself for these problems; after all, the computer is doing the kinds of things computers are supposed to do. What bothers me is the way the computer seems to be so 'superior' and 'in charge,' dictating exactly how things are to be done.

I think one of the reasons I'm particularly bothered by the power of the computer to control what I can and can't do is that it reminds me of the 1968 science fiction movie, "2001 Space Odyssey," in which the computer (HAL) took over the spaceship from the humans on board. While the humans prevailed in the end, it was a very unsettling situation, not unlike the way we have to constantly wrestle with our own personal computers today.

Of course, there's a lesson in the movie that could benefit all of us as we deal with the challenging aspects of the technology we use on a daily basis. The lesson is that we need to learn a good bit about the way the computer works. I've already learned a lot during the past twelve years since I first launched my website. But this work involves lifelong learning because no matter how much you know there are constantly new programs and procedures to be learned along the way. I realize that I'm extremely fortunate to have my own personal computer expert to call on to bail me out. My son is a systems administrator by professional and a guru on all things related to computers.

Whether or not you have a website or only use your computer for email and to surf the Web, there's still a lot to learn—and the first thing is to become familiar with the 'language.' This is a very different language, with words that were not part of our regular vocabulary prior to the advent of computers. The new words include some that can be downright disturbing, words like 'firewall' or 'hacker' or 'virus' or 'trojan.' And then there are the routine words in the computer world, like 'boot' or 'download' or 'IM' or 'blog.'

In the final analysis, we need to balance our complaints about computers with appreciation for the wonderful benefits they make possible. We literally have a world of information at our fingertips. While this is both interesting and enlightening, it can also be lifesaving when used to gain critical medical and lifestyle information.

So the next time you find yourself irritated by the hassles that arise with computer use, you might stop and consider that the trade-offs between the hassles and the benefits weigh heavily in favor of the benefits. Anything worthwhile usually involves investing a good bit of time, energy and thought, and the use of computers is no exception. So let us try to appreciate this wonderful tool that has the ability to improve our lives in so many ways.

# Chapter 12: Freedom and Responsibility

Citizens of the World
Soldiers Serving in Iraq
"The War"
Voting: a Right and a Responsibility
Summons for Jury Duty
Report on Jury Duty
Political Awareness
Remembering the Past
Getting Along

*Freedom and Responsibility*

**Citizens of the World** May 2006

Those of us who live in the U.S. (or any other country that enjoys a great deal of freedom) have a certain responsibility to be informed and aware of what's involved in maintaining our freedoms. It's tempting to try to avoid focusing on some of the painful and difficult activities that make this freedom possible.

I'm typical of those who would prefer not to be exposed to things that 'no one should see.' (Heck, I don't even like to see violent movies that are totally fiction.) But I've forced myself to get past this resistance and go ahead and inform myself about what's happening in the world.

So this commitment to being a responsible citizen led me to watch a documentary that recently aired on HBO titled "Baghdad ER." As the title implies, it was an inside view of the daily work of the medical teams doing the difficult and critical emergency room work in Baghdad.

The scenes in this documentary were chilling, moving, heartwarming—and heartbreaking. They were also the most gruesome images I've ever seen, including the opening sequences in the WW II movie "Saving Private Ryan" that showed the invasion of Normandy. Of course, viewing a film of such events in no way compares to the real thing for those who are on the scene.

My feeling is that if they can *live* this horror, I can at least *watch* it—to know what others are enduring for all the rest of us. I'm making no commentary on the war itself, only encouraging people to step up to your responsibility to be informed citizens about what's happening in the world we live in.

However, my point is not specifically about this one film. It's more an invitation (a challenge?) to *not* protect yourself from being exposed to the events that are happening in the world that ultimately affect us all.

So let me go ahead and mention a few other instances where we can be responsible in knowing what's happening—or what's already happened.

I recently saw the movie "United 93" about the plane that crashed in Pennsylvania on 9/11 due to the heroics of the passengers on board, thereby preventing it from crashing into either the White House or the Capitol. That was hard to watch as well, but I figured if the families of those who died could cooperate with the filming and watch the movie, going to see it was the very least I could do.

Other movies I've seen for the same general reason include "Shindler's List," "Black Hawk Down" and "Hotel Rwanda." (I'm sure there are others, but these are the first ones that come to mind.) Of course, it's not just movies. Recently, I've also watched many excellent TV programs depicting the genocide of the people in Darfur, Sudan, as well as the stories of thousands of children in Africa who lead lives of true desperation.

The point is not to congratulate myself. I'm no stronger or braver than anyone else, and I'm certainly not inclined to suffer unnecessarily, but I feel blessed to have served as a 'witness' to these various depictions of significant world events and circumstances. And I encourage each of you to do as I try to do—suck it up and accept responsibility for knowing what's happening in the world around us.

\* \* \* \* \* \* \* \*

*Freedom and Responsibility*

**Soldiers Serving in Iraq**                      **October 2006**

I recently attended a screening of a documentary called "The Ground Truth," featuring American soldiers who have served in Iraq. Although we read the statistics of the war, this documentary puts a very personal face on the soldiers, particularly for those of us who don't have a loved one serving.

It's obviously quite difficult for them to open up about their experiences. For decades soldiers returning home from wars have quietly tried to deal with their personal demons, seldom sharing even with their friends and family, much less the larger society. So we should feel honored to witness their sharing.

I admit that it's painful to watch, but it's important for us to be aware of the ways in which their lives are changed forever. Regardless of your personal feelings about the war itself, the price paid by these brave young men and women is something we all need to acknowledge and respect.

           \*   \*   \*   \*   \*   \*   \*   \*   \*

**"The War"**                                         **October 2007**

Most of us haven't personally been on the front lines in battle, and only those who have 'been there' really know the realities of war. However, I now have a much better sense of war after watching the 15-hour Ken Burns documentary series on PBS called simply "The War." (It's about World War II, the title reflecting the fact that it's still referred to as 'the Big One.')

Watching this series made war more *real* than anything I've ever seen. It was comprised completely of actual war footage—with no reenactments. And although I've seen a number of war movies, *nothing* comes close to seeing the real thing.

In the years since World War II, there have been a number of wars, but in all of them we got a limited view of what was happening. Those of us who remember Vietnam know that we felt we got a somewhat realistic picture of what was happening there, but it was still quite sanitized compared with the real thing. As a consequence, we have not fully appreciated the reality of what happens on the battlefields.

Perhaps you think you have a pretty good sense of what war is like from the more graphic footage we've seen on TV recently of the fighting in Iraq. But, again, this doesn't give you an accurate picture of the real nature of war. In fact, the only realistic picture of war you're likely to see is contained in the footage from this film, shot about 65 years ago—since more recent war footage won't be shown out of consideration for the privacy of those soldiers and their families who are still suffering the repercussions of their experience.

In addition to a realistic picture of war as it was fought on the battlefront, the series also focused on the loved ones waiting (and worrying) back home. It offers a glimpse into the impact on *all* the people who were affected in some way. However, since the war was fought in almost every country in Europe and Asia, the U.S. was far less affected than all those countries where millions of innocent civilians died.

Frankly, as fewer and fewer of us are directly affected by more recent wars, we desperately need to learn the lessons that are known only by those who have had firsthand experience.

We'd be wise to take heed of a saying attributed to George Santayana: *"Those who cannot learn from history are doomed to repeat it."*

*Freedom and Responsibility*

This series has much to teach us, not just about the past, but about who we are as people of the world. Watching this series provides the kind of perspective that everyone needs if they're to be truly informed about war. Frankly, we don't deserve to have an opinion about anything related to war if we don't have *informed* opinions based on exposing ourselves to the realities of war.

It's not easy to expose ourselves to the harsh realities of many of the world's ills. I acknowledge having to overcome my own resistance to seeing almost every war movie I've seen. But every time I came away with a deeper commitment to overcoming the harsh brutalities that damage and destroy so many people.

\* \* \* \* \* \* \* \* \*

**Voting: a Right and a Responsibility**  November 2006

Tuesday, November 7, is election day in the U.S. While our country strongly supports the idea of people in other countries gaining the right to vote, people in our own country often fail to exercise this right. And in so doing, they're also failing a major responsibility of citizenship.

As with almost all endeavors, rights come with responsibilities. And if we fail to assume our responsibilities, we're in danger of losing our right to influence the course of the events that impact our lives on a daily basis.

So I want to pose a simple question: Do you vote? If so, good for you—and for the country. And if you don't, I invite you to strongly challenge whatever reason (excuse?) you've made that allows you to feel OK about not voting.

Here are a few of the questions that are raised about voting:

1. Does my vote really makes a difference?

With the extremely close presidential elections we've had in recent years in the U.S., it's clear that you never know when a few votes may totally change the outcome of any election.

2. Will the votes be accurately counted?

This is a particularly troubling question with the new electronic voting machines that have no paper trail and have been shown to be able to be 'hacked,' changing votes at will. But just because some votes may be miscounted does not invalidate the whole voting process. It's certainly better than completely giving up the chance to make a difference.

3. Will registering to vote put me on some 'lists'—like the one used for jury duty?

While I don't know the definitive answer to this, it's a moot point since people can be excused from jury duty if they have legitimate reasons for being unable to serve. And those who are able to serve certainly need to be willing to do so.

4. How can I vote when I work long hours and can't make it to the polls?

It's a simple matter to get an absentee ballot. I've gotten one for quite a few years. It's very convenient to be able to quietly mark your ballot in your own home on your own schedule.

I'm sure there are other reasons/excuses that can be given. But the bottom line is that we usually manage to do the things we feel are really important. And voting is one of the most important actions you can take as a citizen of this or any other country.

*Freedom and Responsibility*

So I urge everyone to vote. I also urge you to inform yourselves about the issues and vote based on those candidates who reflect your own positions—rather than along a strict party line. We need to accept our responsibility to participate in the political process if we are to assume our rights as citizens.

\* \* \* \* \* \* \* \* \*

**Summons for Jury Duty** May 2006

Tomorrow I'm to fulfill my civic responsibility by reporting for Jury Duty. When I received the Summons for jury service, I had the initial reaction that many people have: "Why me? Why now?" Of course, there never seems to be a *convenient* time to drop everything else in your life for this command performance. But I do—because I always think of how important it is for every citizen to be 'judged by a jury of their peers.' And we can't reasonably complain about our jury system if we fail to play our part in making it work.

So I go. In fact the jury selection process is a fascinating experience in and of itself. Part of you hopes you won't be chosen (so you can go back to your daily life and regular responsibilities), but another part of you doesn't want to fail to be selected. So it's very hard to respond to questions in a completely straightforward way without overanalyzing the impact of every response you make to questions about who you are and what you do.

Despite my efforts to answer questions in a way that wouldn't exclude me from being chosen, in all my times of reporting for duty, I've only been chosen to serve on juries a couple of times. One trial dealt with a financial matter and the other dealt with a charge of mistreatment at a border crossing.

(Since I live near the U.S. border with Mexico, this is not an uncommon issue.)

Both times I felt I gained a great deal from the experience. While I learned something about each of the areas being addressed, the biggest learning was in the process itself, seeing how you function within a group of people trying to reach consensus on the facts of a particular situation. It's all the more fascinating when you're keenly aware of how any two people can look at the exact same situation—but see it very differently.

If you're interested in one of the best jury movies ever made, check out the original 1957 version of "12 Angry Men." It has an all-star cast, including Henry Fonda, Lee J. Cobb, E. G. Marshall, Jack Klugman, Jack Warden, Martin Balsam, and Ed Begley. And it's one of the most gripping depictions of group dynamics you'll ever find. Since we used to show this movie in corporate training programs we conducted, I've seen it dozens of times. But after receiving this most recent jury summons, I got it out and watched it again.

I doubt that I'll experience anything similar to the drama of that movie. In fact, my experience is likely to be anticlimactic since, as mentioned earlier, I seldom get chosen to serve on a jury. But it feels good simply to do my duty by showing up. So I'm off to Court...

\* \* \* \* \* \* \* \* \*

## Report on Jury Duty    May 2006

Today I reported for jury duty. I went with high hopes of being chosen to serve—since I believe in the importance of doing your civic duty. (Frankly, we can't justifiably criticize the

## Freedom and Responsibility

working of any aspect of our government if we aren't willing to do our part.)

Anyway, I spent eight hours at the Courthouse, the first couple of hours involving orientation and just waiting. Then I was assigned to a courtroom (along with 40 other potential jurors) to be questioned about a criminal case where the charge was 'child abuse and battery with criminal intent.' I was *not* selected to serve.

Actually, I was surprised that I was one of the last jurors to be dismissed before the final 12 were determined. As those who've reported for jury duty know, you're asked a lot of personal questions about your general life situation (occupation, spouse and kids, their occupations, etc.) You're also asked many questions relevant to the specific case—to determine whether you can be a fair and impartial juror.

While I would've tried my best to be open-minded and assess the case according to the law, I was completely candid about both my experience and thoughts on various aspects of 'physical discipline' (as it was referred to in the questioning of potential jurors).

You see, I have a long-standing belief that physical discipline is neither necessary nor effective. In fact, many years ago I wrote a regular column for a local child care newsletter—and one of my pieces was on 'spanking.' (I'm opposed to it, as are most child development experts.) One of the clearest ways of expressing this was a bumper sticker I once saw that said, *"People are not for hitting. Children are people too."*

Anyway, I'm sure it was clear to the attorneys that it would be difficult for me to impartially assess a case involving physical discipline, especially when it was charged as being quite excessive (choking, among other things). I do believe in 'innocent until proven guilty,' but when the head and heart are fighting, I know it would've been a struggle, despite my best efforts to remain objective.

Nevertheless, I felt good about getting another glimpse into the workings of our justice system. And I was very impressed with the caliber of the other potential jurors in the room with me. They represented a wide range of ages from a wide range of backgrounds and life experiences. It seemed that everyone was like me, genuinely trying to be as open and straightforward as possible.

So if you've ever tried to avoid jury duty, I hope you'll reconsider and use it as an opportunity to learn a lot—not only about our system of justice, but also about yourself and your fellow citizens.

\* \* \* \* \* \* \* \* \*

**Political Awareness**                                             **January 2007**

This past week has been filled with political news—from the U.S. President's State of the Union speech (with the first female Speaker of the House seated behind him) to the announcements from several candidates that they're 'throwing their hats in the ring' for the 2008 presidential campaign.

Since I'm a news junkie myself, I'm always surprised at how many people are basically unaware of political events. Unfortunately, I think a lot of people (including myself, at times) are so discouraged at the political partisanship, the influence of lobbyists, and the campaign finance issues that they simply tune out all the chatter about politics and government.

However, it seems that when living in a country like the U.S. where our government is declared to be "of the people, by

*Freedom and Responsibility*

the people, for the people," everyone would be particularly interested in what's happening—especially since everyone depends on government in one way or another to provide valuable services. But many don't know much about how government operates and may not even know the names of our leaders—much less leaders of other key countries in the world. It seems that with so much at stake, it behooves us all to pay attention to what's going on.

Just last week I had an interesting experience in observing some who were (and some who were not) conscious of politicians and their actions. I heard a couple of adults react to comments about some political places/events in a way that indicated they knew nothing about them. On the other hand, I heard a group of 11-year-old girls discussing politicians and world events with a degree of awareness that was quite knowledgeable, sensible, and impressive.

Of course, in households where politics and world events are routinely discussed, kids are likely to be much more aware than in households where the focus is only on their own neighborhood and their personal activities. So even if adults are not interested in world events themselves, they need to prepare their children to live in the truly global environment they will inherit—where their survival may depend on being aware and involved in political realities.

Therefore, I encourage everyone (for their own sake and for the sake of the children) to become more aware of (and informed about) politics, government, and world events. While it may be difficult and discouraging at times, it's *there*, affecting all our lives.

\* \* \* \* \* \* \* \* \*

## Remembering the Past            January 2008

Just when we think (or hope) we're making great progress in race relations in the U.S., we get reminded of the disastrous injustices done to 'blacks' in the past—most notable among the many abuses being the common practice of 'lynching.'

While we need to remember the past atrocities against African Americans, the remembering needs to be in the context of trying to heal from these wounds. But that's not possible when people continue to bring it up in completely insensitive, thoughtless, even lighthearted ways.

This is what happened recently when a reporter (Kelly Tilghman) on the Golf Channel made an off-the-cuff remark about 'lynching' Tiger Woods to prevent his seemingly unstoppable power to beat his competition. She subsequently apologized for 'some poorly chosen words.'

Tiger's spokesman issued a statement saying, *"Regardless of the choice of words used, we know unequivocally that there was no ill intent in her comments."* However, as pointed out by DeWayne Wickham in one of his columns in USA Today, *"But he's wrong. This is a much bigger issue than either Woods or his spokesman is able to imagine."*

Yes, this *is* a big deal—because casual references to lynchings just add insult to injury and diminish the significance of these atrocities of the past. We need to acknowledge the damage that was done and to reflect on this period of our history in a way that moves us forward rather than pulling us backwards.

This whole issue is a very sensitive one for me since I was born and raised in Mississippi. I haven't lived there in over 45 years, but I still have the accent and am concerned about being seen as a stereotypical person who doesn't care about the past.

*Freedom and Responsibility*

I feel a personal responsibility to do whatever I can to make up for the history of my ancestors and all those who behaved in such inhumane ways.

In fact, I make a point of *reminding* myself of the past as a way of not forgetting what needs to be done in the future to heal the wounds from that time. One recent reminder came from watching the extraordinary film "The Great Debaters," a true story about a small black Texas college that beat Harvard in a debate in 1935. Integral to the story was the depiction of the lynching and burning of a black man, searing this image into the memory of other blacks who observed these atrocities.

We'd do well as current-day citizens to deliberately face these images and other reminders of our tortured past when it comes to race relations. You may want to avoid focusing on such a painful time in the past, but to forget is to risk further harm in the future. So let us remember that the very word 'lynching' is a trigger back to that time and has no place in casual conversation, only in serious discussions about the need to continue healing from this painful period in our history.

* * * * * * * * *

**Getting Along** September 2007

These are sobering times—when many factions around the world are battling each other over their beliefs. But I guess it's not surprising that various countries can't get along, when people *within* individual countries can't seem to get along either. While Iraq quickly comes to mind in that context, unfortunately, it's also still true in the U.S.—even though we like to see ourselves as having moved beyond slavery, the Civil War, racial injustice, etc.

My focus on this issue began last week when my oldest granddaughter interviewed me for a course assignment in conjunction with studying the book, "To Kill a Mockingbird." The assignment was to interview someone who read the book and/or saw the movie back in 1960 and 1962 when they first appeared—to ask about the nature of the public reaction to the story 'at that time.'

The setting for the book was the deep South in the early 1930s, and it was based on a couple of true cases in 1919 and 1937. Although I wasn't born until 1936, I'd grown up in the South. And even though I no longer lived there when the movie came out, I was concerned that others would think *all* Southerners were racist. Not only was I embarrassed to be a Southerner, but I was horrified at the gross injustice to blacks that the movie portrayed.

Anyway, I shared all my thoughts about that time with my granddaughter, then pointed out to her that we still have serious issues around racial injustice in the U.S. I told her about the current situation with the 'Jena 6.' (It's called Jena 6 because it involves the legal case of 6 black teenagers in Jena, Louisiana, who had several altercations with some white kids.)

My granddaughter was aghast that racial antagonisms and racial injustice were still this kind of issue today—and that her history assignment was as much about 'current events' as about 'history.'

As for me, when I observe my granddaughters and their friends (where they embrace everyone equally, without noting racial or ethnic differences), it gives me hope that we'll eventually see the day when they will lead the way in providing a positive response to Rodney King's 1991 call, *"Can't we all just get along?"*

# Chapter 13: Making a Difference

      Doing Good in the World
      Helping Others
      Giving and Receiving
      Patience and Persistence
      Help in Times of Crisis
      Pay it Forward
      Supporting those in Crisis
      Giving—Large and Small

*Making a Difference*

**Doing Good in the World** June 2006

I tend to be a very serious person—you might even say *too* serious. Part of that may come from the fact that I'm such a news junkie and keep up with many of the disturbing events taking place all over the world. But in addition to all the horrible stories I hear, I also hear about the wonderful, inspiring efforts of ordinary people doing extraordinary things—people who are making a difference. From these stories, it's clear that each of us can contribute in some way to making a difference in the world.

I do somewhat offset my serious take on the world by also being a trivia junkie in that I keep up with a lot of the reporting about the world of entertainment. This means I know a good bit (sometimes more than I really care to know) about the lives of celebrities. But often that also means learning about the causes to which they contribute their time and money.

This week, my two worlds collided in an interesting way—when I focused on a couple of extraordinary efforts on the part of some celebrities in making a difference. Anyone (mostly women, my husband tells me) who has kept up with the frenzy over the birth of Brad Pitt and Angelina Jolie's baby knows that they chose to sell the baby's first photos for millions—and give it all to charity.

Of course, many celebrities donate money to various causes, which is nice, but this donation is even more impressive because it's just an extension of the time and effort they personally invest in their philanthropic work. For instance, Angelina is a goodwill ambassador for the U.N. on Refugees and they both spend a lot of time and energy working directly with the people they're trying to help. They make a point of using their celebrity to draw attention to the plight of people, particularly children, in impoverished countries around the world.

Of course, this latest example of using your celebrity to make a difference on an ongoing basis is not new. One of the best and most outstanding examples is the work of Paul Newman, who has for many years raised millions of dollars for charity through his Newman's Own array of products. He even allows the products to carry his photo (which goes against his personal preferences), but he does it for the sake of sales that raise more money for his charity efforts.

Actually, focusing at this particular time on Paul Newman's efforts also came through the intersection of my serious and silly sides—the movie "Cars," in which Paul Newman plays a major role. Another confession: I greatly enjoyed this movie, not only for the story line extolling the virtues of the simple life, but also because I've been a Nascar fan for the past twelve years, even attending several races with my son.

Anyway, the point of this discussion is to remind you (as I'm reminding myself) that we can find good being done by many different people in many different places—and *all* of us can do our part in contributing to the ongoing need for making a difference in the world.

ADDENDUM: September 26, 2008. Paul Newman lost his battle with cancer at the age of 83. The news was filled with many well-deserved tributes to his acting—*and* to his generous philanthropy.

\* \* \* \* \* \* \* \* \*

*Making a Difference*

**Helping Others**                                                   **January 2007**

I get a great deal of inspiration from stories of people who have gone out of their way to help others, especially when it's been at personal sacrifice. One of the most dramatic (and unbelievable) stories was a recent situation where a man in a New York subway station saved the life of a stranger who had fallen on the tracks by jumping on top of him and holding him down between the tracks while the train passed a few inches above them.

Appropriately, he was rewarded with praise, gifts and special recognition as a hero—although his actions certainly were not motivated by those rewards. They were the actions of a man bent on helping others. And in his interviews he repeatedly said it was simply the kind of thing people should do.

Most of us will never be called on to risk our lives for the sake of others—as this man and thousands of our young men and women do every day in the military. But all of us can do 'random acts of kindness' as we go about our daily lives.

I must admit that helping others is one of my greatest joys, not because I'm such a *good* person; it's because I feel so much better about myself when I know I've been helpful to someone else. I especially enjoy helping strangers—partly because it's so freely given, not something that's expected of me. Simply doing whatever we're *expected* to do somehow doesn't bring the same degree of satisfaction.

So if you're feeling low and struggling with some particularly difficult problem (as all of us do from time to time), one of the best antidotes to the feelings of hopelessness or helplessness is simply doing something for someone else.

When we're thinking of others, we can't be as absorbed in our own 'stuff.'

\* \* \* \* \* \* \* \* \*

**Giving and Receiving**                                            **March 2007**

There's a verse in the old testament of the Christian Bible that says, "It is more blessed to give than to receive." Unfortunately, some of us take that message much too far—and I include myself among those misguided people. I continue to learn (over and over again) that it's also blessed to *receive*—because receiving allows others the pleasure and satisfaction of giving.

Now that I'm a parent and grandparent, I think back on how misguided I was in refusing my daddy's financial help when I was newly married and we were struggling while in college. He worked very hard for what little he had, but he took great pride in periodically giving us a little money. Knowing it was difficult for him, I often resisted his efforts. But now I can clearly see that my resisting was denying or diminishing the great pleasure he got out of helping us.

This difficulty in receiving continues to be a problem for me even today. For instance, there was just such an incident last month when my children and grandchildren made a big deal out of celebrating my birthday. I couldn't deny the grandchildren, so I didn't resist them, but I actually insisted that my son not get me a gift. He respected my wishes on that day, but subsequently gave me a gift anyway—and I apologized for having been 'difficult' in the first place.

I think I understand some of the basis for my discomfort in letting people give to me. I grew up where money was very tight, and I still vividly recall references to the fact that my mother went without a winter coat so that I could have one. These early experiences continue to influence me today.

Of course, I know better than to blame my current attitudes/behaviors on my childhood. I agree with the following saying from T.A. (Transactional Analysis).

*"You are not your past, but you are a product of it. Who you are may be your parents' fault, but if you stay that way, it's your own fault."*

It seems that women are particularly prone to a tendency to be givers and helpers, but are not as gracious in receiving from others. So I hope those of you who recognize yourselves in my experience will also try to pause to realize that we're *also* giving when we receive; we're giving others the pleasure and satisfaction of giving to us.

\* \* \* \* \* \* \* \* \*

**Patience and Persistence**  **August 2007**

It's tempting to give up if you make an effort and fail to achieve some particular goal, but the real winners are those with the patience and persistence to continue making an effort—despite the setbacks.

The most recent (and one of the most striking) examples of someone who persisted in trying to achieve her goal is a woman named Barbara Morgan. Today (August 8, 2007) she was part of the crew launched into space aboard the shuttle Endeavour. While being an astronaut and going into space is, in and of itself, a great accomplishment requiring a great deal of patience and persistence, her journey demonstrates an even greater degree of determination than most.

You see, she was the backup to Christa McAuliffe (the first teacher in space) back in 1986. The Challenger space shuttle, with Christa McAuliffe aboard, exploded soon after liftoff. By any standard it was a terrible tragedy, made all the more poignant by the fact that school children all over the world were watching—because it had a 'teacher' on board. (Neither Christa nor Barbara were astronauts; they were regular classroom teachers who went through sufficient training to be allowed to fly in space.)

After the Challenger disaster, Barbara went back to the classroom, but she never gave up her dream of going into space. So in 1998 she returned to NASA, completing regular astronaut training and becoming a full-time astronaut. She was scheduled to go into space in 2004, but was subjected to another delay due to the fact that all shuttle flights were grounded after the loss of Columbia in 2003. Now, at age 55, she has achieved her goal of going into space, the culmination of an effort that spans 21 years!

It's easy to get discouraged when we don't reach our goals—particularly if we've made a gallant effort over a period of time. But Barbara Morgan's 21-year dream of going into space became a reality only because of her patience and persistence in making it happen.

Her story serves as an example and an inspiration to all of us *not* to give up if our initial efforts don't succeed. And it doesn't have to be some grand goal like flying in space. For instance, almost everyone at some point in their lives attempts to succeed at basic lifestyle changes like losing weight or stopping smoking or maintaining an exercise program. It's a mistake to assume that failing at the first (or second or third) attempt means it's hopeless. Most of the people who eventually succeed are those who were willing to keep trying.

*Making a Difference*

The proverb *"If at first you don't succeed, try, try again"* is one we've all heard, but, like another proverb, *"It's easier said than done."* When we've tried something that failed to turn out the way we hoped or expected, there's a tendency to give up and comfort ourselves with the idea that at least we tried. But almost every person who has succeeded in any significant way is a person who has also failed numerous times prior to their success.

A prime example of this is Abraham Lincoln, whose failures prior to becoming President of the U.S. are legendary. Here's a list of some of his many failures:

—He failed as a business man—as a storekeeper.

—He failed as a farmer—he despised this work.

—He failed in his first attempt to obtain political office.

—He failed when he sought the office of speaker while in the legislature.

—He failed in his first attempt to go to Congress.

—He failed when he sought an appointment to the United States Land

Office.

—He failed when he ran for the United States Senate.

—He failed when he sought the nomination for the Vice-Presidency in 1856.

Then in 1860, he sought to become President of the U.S.—and he succeeded!

Throughout history, those who achieved the most success were usually those who repeatedly tried and failed—before finally succeeding in some spectacular way. So I hope you'll take another look at some effort you abandoned after it didn't initially work out the way you hoped and consider making another (better, smarter, more concentrated) effort to reach your goal. As reflected in yet another common proverb, *"Nothing ventured, nothing gained."*

\* \* \* \* \* \* \* \* \*

**Help in Times of Crisis**　　　　　　　　　　**October 2007**

This is a time of crisis where I live in Southern California due to the raging wildfires that are ravaging this area. One definition of a crisis is 'an unstable or crucial time'—which accurately describes the situation here this week.

Personally, my family is OK, although my daughter and her family did have to evacuate and briefly stayed here with us. Since their house burned down in the Cedar Fire that swept through this area in 2003, we're quite thankful it was spared this time.

But, as with any natural disaster, everyone is affected in some way. We're all asked to stay off the roads unless necessary, to limit use of cell phones (to clear the channels for the cell phones of rescue workers), and to limit use of electricity since so many power lines are down.

Another indicator of the seriousness of the situation is that many things (from the Court System to the School System to some Starbucks) are closed. Even the media has gone into a highly unusual mode of operation. For the past three days, all four TV network affiliate stations broadcast *no* regular national shows, focusing only on reporting on the fire—and all without commercials!

However, what I want to highlight is the amazing help provided by everyone, both officials and citizens. By all accounts, it's the exact opposite of what happened with Katrina. In fact, I think everyone has learned from the gross mistakes with Katrina—because here you hear nothing but praise for the response from leaders: local, state, and federal.

And local officials also learned from the 2003 Cedar Fire—where there was no integrated communication system and most people were unable to get good information. For instance, this time they were set up with an emergency 'reverse 911 system.' This is a system whereby you don't call 911; they call you—to let you know when to evacuate. This relieved the kind of uncertainty that was so devastating in the earlier fire. It also provided the opportunity for most people to load their most important possessions (photos, papers, etc.) before leaving home.

The most striking thing about the help being provided is that it goes far beyond the basics: food, water, and sleeping accommodations. It's the thousands of small acts of kindness that are so impressive. For instance, some firefighters and police who've seen that a house can't be saved have gone in and removed family photos from the walls, tagging them with the address to hold for residents later on. This is particularly appreciated by those people who had to evacuate in the middle of the night with very little warning due to unexpected wind shifts.

About 500,000 people have been evacuated from their homes in the San Diego area, and many are staying with friends or family or in local hotels and motels. However, all hotels and motels are at full occupancy (and not everyone can afford to stay in a hotel), so a large number of people are taking refuge in Qualcomm Stadium. Those at the stadium are being well-served by contributions from the business community. In fact, the outpouring of help is so overwhelming that it goes beyond what can be used. For instance, much of the food is spoiling because the restaurants are taking more food to the stadium than can be consumed; so they're being asked to stop bringing it.

The kinds of help being provided cover a wide variety of goods and services, including cots, tents, clothes, toiletries, towels, mobile showers, medical services, counseling, live entertainment, yoga groups, and even AA meetings. They also have access to television so they can keep up with the unfolding story and to get updated information. While far from normal, it's a kind of temporary city with many of the amenities of normal life.

And citizens have been providing an enormous amount of help. Many volunteers have descended on the stadium (a ratio of about one volunteer for every ten people), including people from all walks of life. Many are among those whose workplaces are closed, some are students from local colleges that are closed, and some are from among the evacuees themselves who are stepping up to volunteer in helping the whole operation.

The bottom line is that you hear no complaints or criticism of anything or anybody regarding the way this whole endeavor is being organized and implemented. It's sure to stand as a shining example of the right way to provide help in times of crisis. And it serves as a guide for the kind of helping attitude that could be adopted by all of us in conducting our daily lives, even when there's no major crisis.

\* \* \* \* \* \* \* \* \*

## Pay it Forward October 2007

This phrase, 'pay it forward' was coined by Robert A. Heinlein in a book published in 1951. But I only became aware of it

## Making a Difference

(and of its meaning) when I saw a movie by that title that came out in 2000.

Pay it forward refers to repaying the good deeds one has received by doing good things for other unrelated people. In other words, when someone helps you in some way—don't pay it back, pay it forward by helping someone else.

I'm thinking about this concept at this point because it relates to my previous column about the Southern California wild fires. Now that the fires are over, people are trying to pick up the pieces of their lives, and they're being assisted by a group of people who are paying it forward.

As I mentioned earlier, my daughter and her family lost their house in the 2003 California wild fires. They've since rebuilt, but they went through several years of intense difficulty in dealing with all the practical and emotional hassles involved replacing *everything*!

One thing that made a tremendous difference was the outpouring of help and support from others who did everything possible to help ease the way for them. This was particularly important in the first few weeks and months when people didn't even have the basics of life. One community group set up a center where burned-out families could show up and simply take whatever they needed in the way of clothes, toys, basic household items, etc.

There were 300 families in my daughter's neighborhood who lost their homes in the 2003 fire, and they banded together to stay in touch and to swap tips about how to deal with the multitude of issues they all faced. This continued to be their lifeline as they worked through the maze of bureaucratic red tape involved in everything from re-establishing their identity to their rebuilding efforts.

They've continued to maintain their email contact since that time, offering encouragement and strength in dealing with the fallout from their joint experiences. Now they're stepping in to help the current fire victims by providing practical items based on immediate needs.

But, more importantly, they've organized an effort to help the new fire victims by sharing all that they learned from their experiences in going through the same ordeal.

They're providing insights and perspective on all the details of getting through the maze of issues to be addressed. For instance, they're preparing file boxes with folders already labeled for the various areas that will need attention, many of them areas the new victims don't yet know they'll need.

In fact, when current fire victims gather at centers where a number of different agencies have set up tables to help them, the longest line by far is the one at the table manned by the 2003 fire victims who've had personal experience with what these people are going through now.

This kind of person-to-person support is a special service that is invaluable. This is a classic case where no one can fully understand or appreciate the toll of any specific tragedy unless they have been there.

We see this is many areas—where people who've already suffered some kind of setback in life use their experience to help others. Frankly, while this kind of help is beneficial for the people who are receiving the help, it's also extremely beneficial for the people doing the helping. Using your experience to help others helps you feel strong and confident after going through a time when you may have felt weak and out of control. So it's a win-win for all concerned.

Nothing feels better than taking a bad situation and turning it into something useful. And since almost everyone faces some kind of crisis in their lives, you might reflect on whatever crisis you've faced—and consider ways you might use what you learned from that experience to help others. Sometimes 'helping others' is also the best way to 'help yourself.' If you failed to get help when you needed it, you can still start the process by helping someone else. And if you *were* helped by others, then you might consider seeking ways that you can Pay it Forward.

\* \* \* \* \* \* \* \* \*

**Supporting those in Crisis**                                          **October 2006**

'Life is difficult.' This is the opening line of M. Scott Peck's book, "The Road Less Traveled." This statement is quite true in the sense that most of us face one or more genuine crises during our lives.

These kinds of crises may involve the death of a loved one or any other kind of significant loss. And at such times we need the comfort and support of those who care for us, but even more valuable is having the support of others who've 'been there' and can therefore better understand the struggle to deal with the crisis.

Since many of us have difficulty fully comprehending the sense of loss involved in this kind of situation, I want to share a message that was distributed by the fire survivors that reflects their ongoing struggle to cope with their loss and describes the need for others to better understand what they're feeling in recovering from this crisis.

Here's the message shared by the fire survivors:

## MUSINGS ON LIFE

"PLEASE DON'T CALL US LUCKY
   We live with our losses. Well-meaning people say, "Aren't you lucky? You have a new home and new things!" Yet they don't understand why our faces don't instantly share their sympathetic joy and why our voices subtly change.
   We 'Firefolk' can say we are lucky, if we so choose on any given day. But when others say it, to many of us it feels as if they discount our loss, and don't recognize our personal costs, counting us only as alive or dead while envying our new acquisitions...no matter how hard it may have been to endure rebuilding our lives.
   Most days in the present we are glad: it was just stuff. Life is all that matters, and we savor it.
   But when we grieve our lost keepsakes, our pets, our love-letters, or we are told that insurance won't fully cover our losses; when we cannot sit back and enjoy the videotapes of kids growing up, or when we feel we have been a burden to friends and family—then we don't feel lucky at all! At those times we feel like innocent victims of fate's wrath!
   Some devastated neighbors revealed that they even had days where they wished they had died rather than live like they did that first year. So please...don't tell them they were lucky they were not injured or killed.

   —Tell them instead that you are glad they are still here, and let them know why.
   —Tell them that you care about their grief, their pain, their anger and their adjustments.
   —Tell them you will willingly rehear their disappointments, their losses and their frustrations.
   —And have patience while they relearn to live.

*Then someday we all can tell you how lucky we are—to have someone like you who understands and accepts our sorrows and who also shares our newfound joys!"*

I hope this message will be helpful to all of us who want to be more effective in our responses to people dealing with any kind of loss.

\* \* \* \* \* \* \* \* \*

**Giving—Large and Small**                                  **July 2006**

You've probably seen the headlines saying, "The second-richest man in the world [Warren Buffet] is giving 31 billion dollars to the richest man in the world [Bill Gates]." However, that really misses the main point—which is that Warren Buffet is giving 31 billion dollars to help the children of the world. The Bill and Melinda Gates Foundation is simply the avenue through which the philanthropy will take place.

I watched the Charlie Rose Show do a series of four interviews with Warren Buffet and Bill and Melinda Gates. This close relationship between the world's two richest men is quite fascinating. And while the friendship and the trust they've developed is interesting and admirable, the personal focus on the two of them somewhat diminishes the focus on the significance of the effort they're making to address their joint belief that all children are valuable and deserve equity in this world—not being penalized by the random luck of where in the world they happen to be born. (Buffet refers to this as the 'ovarian lottery.')

This is such a powerful, compassionate way to look at people—one that is in short supply in an age where there's so much focus on 'me and mine.' But anyone who has been paying attention recognizes that we're in a global situation now where we're affected by everything that happens to anyone in any area of the world. As we see from so much terrorist activity, there is no *safe* place anymore—and it's actually in our own best interests to try to bring as much equity as possible to the opportunities available for everyone.

At the very least, we can work to 'save the children,' which is the goal of the joint effort of these particular people. Of course, Bill and Melinda Gates began their Foundation in 1999 and their current endowment was already 29.2 billion before adding the Buffet contribution. In fact, by more than doubling the endowment, they believe that their joint efforts will soon result in an estimated 10 million children being alive who would otherwise have died.

The Foundation supports efforts to prevent and treat diseases and conditions that meet three criteria:
(1) they cause widespread illness and death in developing countries
(2) they represent the greatest inequities in health between developed and developing countries
(3) they receive inadequate attention and funding.

The primary diseases include tuberculosis, malaria, HIV/AIDS, acute diarrhea, vaccine-preventable diseases, and other infectious diseases. And recognizing that the medicine does no good if the children don't have food to eat, they also work in that area as well.

They're trying to improve the conditions for children all over the world, including the U.S., starting by assessing their primary current needs. So while 60% of the Foundation's philanthropy goes toward the health of children in underdeveloped countries, the other 40% goes toward improving education in the U.S. The more dramatic work

## Making a Difference

overseas often overshadows the work in the U.S., but they're equally committed to investing in the children of the U.S. in providing the basics to succeed in school and life.

Watching these extraordinarily wealthy people demonstrate such care and concern for those less fortunate has helped to soften my lifelong bias against those who are 'well-off' (as we used to call it when I was growing up in the South). As a family that was not at all well-off, I was clearly aware of issues between the 'haves' and the 'have-nots.' As I've written before, my Daddy worked in a stave mill while I was growing up. Then in my late teens he got a service station, which he continued to operate until his death.

Growing up, Daddy was the oldest boy in a family of nine and dropped out of school in the tenth grade to help support the family, then educated himself by reading the encyclopedia. I was extremely proud of him and of his appreciation for life and his compassion for others. Despite the fact that he had very little, he always gave to everyone around him, particularly every child who came into his service station—which was back in the day when there was no 'self-serve' and he interacted with every customer in this small Mississippi town.

So while I have enormous respect for the way Buffet and the Gates are using the fruits of their own good fortune to help others, I'm certainly not putting them on a pedestal above those of lesser means who do what they can. For instance, even with their enormous giving, it won't have a noticeable effect on their own personal lifestyles. So I have a special respect for those who have much less, but give what they can, often diminishing the lifestyle they can afford to sustain.

Of course, even more significant than the monetary giving is the giving of time and energy (which anyone can do) in meeting face-to-face with those you're trying to help. So I'm particularly struck by these very wealthy people constantly visiting the needy children in the areas of the world they're trying to serve and seeing up close and personal just what's required and what difference they can make.

I know from my own experience that simply *knowing* about a problem is not the same as spending time involved in it. Most of us have done some kind of 'helping others' during our lives, but the most significant one for me was my very first major work—as a Housemother in a Children's Home when I was only 21. This experience informed me in so many ways and gave me an invaluable appreciation for the importance of home and family.

# Chapter 14: The Big Picture

Our Planet's Past
Global Warming
Nowhere to Hide
Out of this World
Where All Things Belong
We're All in this Together
The Whole World

*The Big Picture*

## Our Planet's Past                    July 2006

I live in San Diego, home of the world-renowned San Diego Zoo. But the zoo is nestled in a larger area called Balboa Park—which includes, among other things, a number of excellent museums. I hadn't been to the museums in quite awhile, but I went one day last week when several of the museums were open to the public for free. One of them was the Museum of Natural History, which I'd visited several times with my granddaughters.

Unexpectedly, this time I found a new exhibit that literally took my breath away. It was a very large globe, depicting the Plant Earth as it evolved over the past six hundred million years! At the beginning of the sequence, all the land masses were together. As the time-clock moved through the years, the land masses gradually shifted—moving apart, then back together in different configurations.

These transitions made the earth appear to be pulsating— like the living organism that it is. As the changes continued toward more recent times, you could see the present-day configuration of continents take form.

It took three or four times of watching the entire sequence to position myself in a way to see just how the development took place. I'd love to have seen it go from present day back to the beginning so I could have more easily traced back the different positions.

Anyway, it was absolutely mesmerizing. I think I could've watched it all day. Actually, this was much the same reaction I had when I saw the first photo of earth that was taken from space—awed at the beauty and the fragile nature of this planet we call home.

And since I recently saw "An Inconvenient Truth," the documentary about global warming, I found myself musing about how much I wish all the people of the world could more clearly recognize how we're all in this together. This is our only home, and it's important that we take care of it—and of each other.

Actually, I think the focus on saving the planet misses the bigger issue. The 'planet' is likely to go on long after we cause it to be uninhabitable for our form of life. So the real challenge is to save the *people* of the planet.

Frankly, in the context of this larger view of the planet, all the territorial disputes and wars between countries seem extraordinarily shortsighted and self-destructive. Just as viewing earth from space means you don't see the boundaries between countries, viewing the huge Plant Earth ball at the Museum means that over time you can't even see fixed continents, much less distinct countries.

I wish everyone could get this larger perspective of our planet and our place in relation to it. The world would certainly be a different (better, more peaceful, more compassionate) place to live—plus we'd be more likely to sustain life on the planet for those who will follow us in the millions of years to come.

\* \* \* \* \* \* \* \* \*

### Global Warming                           July 2006

I really enjoy warm weather, but no one enjoys the kind of oppressive heat currently dominating the Northern hemisphere of our planet. Many people are suffering due to the torrid weather that blankets the entire U.S. and many other countries

## The Big Picture

around the world. People are not just uncomfortable; many are dying from the effects of the heat.

Unfortunately, this is not likely to be an unusual situation in the coming years. Many scientists have been warning about the impact of global warming on our climate for a long time, but the issue has been a source of a good bit of public debate.

However, the public in general is now taking notice of this crisis in a much more serious way. And if recent scientific information is to be trusted, the 'debate' is over—and it's time for action. Even if someone is not convinced, it's smart to err on the side of protecting our planet rather than hoping the scientists are wrong.

If anyone still doubts the reality and the scope of this problem, there are many excellent sources of information, beginning with Al Gore's documentary, "An Inconvenient Truth."

As is obvious from the reports about global warming, there's a great deal at stake beyond the kind of increasing temperatures we're experiencing this summer. It affects the life of many species, other serious weather issues, and most of all, the coastlines as they currently exist in all the countries of the world. Many coastal cities are on a path to being under water within hundreds—not thousands—of years.

While the first step in addressing this problem is to become better informed, the next step is to focus on the question of what can be *done* about it. While the government's role in changing laws and regulations is a critical component, there's also a challenge for all of us to learn more about the changes we can make in our own lifestyles that can help in moving toward a solution. Like the old quote from journalist Sydney J. Harris, "If you're not part of the solution, you're part of the problem."

Another issue that involves all of us relates to our use of gasoline and the need to move toward alternative methods of running our automobiles. Electric cars are just one of the alternatives. There are also a number of different types of hybrid cars, including plug-in hybrids as well as hybrids that run on ethanol, biodiesel, or hydrogen.

So as we sit and swelter in this heat, let's keep in mind that the climate changes (and the heat waves that accompany them) are likely to be repeated each year in the future—unless and until we learn more and *do* more to address the aspects of this issue that are related to the impact of our behavior on the climate.

\* \* \* \* \* \* \* \* \*

**Nowhere to Hide** April 2007

As I watched the news reports of the shooting at Virginia Tech, I was struck by the desperate circumstances of those who tried to hide under turned-over desks to avoid the gunman's bullets. And it occurred to me (again) that in the world today there's 'nowhere to hide' when confronted by the many threatening situations that occur when least expected.

We understandably worry about the safety of our military men and women deployed in dangerous parts of the world. And we worry about any situation that we know is high risk. We also correctly assume that school is one of the safest places for our children. However, as was clear with the Virginia Tech tragedy and other school shootings in the past, there's no completely safe place anymore.

The situation is reminiscent of the old song by Martha and the Vandellas, "Nowhere to run, nowhere to hide."

## The Big Picture

There once was a time when we thought if we lived in a 'safe' neighborhood or a 'peaceful' country, we could avoid the kind of fear and anxiety confronting people living in more dangerous areas. But just as everyone is impacted by the effects of global warming on our climate, everyone is affected by the growing climate of violence throughout the world.

Rather than being paralyzed by fear and anxiety, we need to recognize that since everyone is vulnerable to being impacted by violence, we must cooperate in reducing the amount of violence in the world at large, not just in our own back yards.

I've seen a dramatic change since I was a child when I could safely go anywhere in my small town on my own. And even when my children were young, we found a place to raise them where they had a measure of freedom, while still being safe. But as I look at the world my grandchildren are growing up in, I see a tremendous difference. They have almost no ability to venture outside their own homes and yards without being exposed to potentially dangerous situations.

So whatever we can do to reduce the negative forces that influence people to turn on their fellow human beings can benefit not just them, but each of us as well. The 'have-nots' will always try to take from the 'haves' unless we actively work toward more equity in our concern for and treatment of those who feel disadvantaged or disenfranchised.

Of course, no circumstances ever warrant the kind of violent outburst we witnessed at Virginia Tech, but we can no longer pretend that we can hide from the ramifications of a failure of society as a whole to address whatever issues reinforce a person's violent tendencies. Closing our doors won't achieve anywhere near the same effect as opening our hearts to the need for all people to be cared for, encouraged and supported in finding a way to feel they're a part of the world rather than separate from it.

* * * * * * * * *

**Out of this World**                                           **June 2007**

I've had a lifelong fascination with space and I never tire of seeing or reading about space-related events. In fact, my interest has intensified in recent years since my oldest granddaughter has shown an interest in such things.

The latest in a series of events we've shared was watching the landing of the shuttle Atlantis after it took supplies to the international space station. We watched the landing 'live' on NASA's website, but it took on a more local element due to the fact that weather conditions in Florida led to shifting the landing site to Edwards Air Base here in Southern California.

Although we were watching the landing on the computer monitor, we heard and felt the sonic boom when the shuttle broke the sound barrier above us. This was a reminder of the specialness of actually attending a launch or a landing—which I experienced about 25 years ago in Florida. I still vividly recall the amazing feeling of the way the ground shook as the rocket lifted off the launch pad.

I do think that focusing on space can remind us of the importance of what we do here on earth. For instance, one of my all-time favorite photos is the famous picture of earth taken from space. From that perspective, there are no boundaries, nothing to divide us as people.

Some of John Lennon's lyrics in "Imagine" capture this sentiment:

## The Big Picture

*"Imagine there's no countries. It isn't hard to do. Nothing to kill or die for... a brotherhood of man. Imagine all the people, sharing all the world..."*

With so much turmoil in the world, we certainly need to pay more attention to the fact that on this planet we're all in this together. Since what we do now will determine the fate of everyone on earth, it's critical that we focus less on our differences and more on the kind of world we want to leave for our children, grandchildren and generations to come.

We not only need to take care of the planet so that it can sustain life for many years in the future, we also need to continue to explore space as an alternate home when the earth will no longer be inhabitable when our sun finally burns out.

For those interested in the 'big picture' of our planet, it was formed about 4.5 billion years ago and is expected to exist another 5 billion years before the death of our sun—and thus of the earth. (Note that this long timeline is no excuse for complacency.)

So in addition to the inspirational aspects of space efforts (like seeing our planet from afar), there's a very practical aspect to building the space station. It's part of a very long-term strategy of making it possible to travel to other planets—and eventually to other galaxies.

Focusing on space does not come as naturally today for large parts of the world's populations living in cities where bright lights hide the stars from view. For instance, as a child, I lived in a small town where the stars were easily visible on most nights, but now I visit our local Planetarium in order to see a replica of the night sky. I want to urge everyone to find ways to maintain a connection to the sky and the universe as a whole—and to instill this interest in younger generations.

For instance, here are some ideas—based on my own efforts to perpetuate a focus on the importance of space. When she was very young, I gave my oldest granddaughter a small telescope, and over the years she's enjoyed several opportunities to look through more powerful telescopes. I've also taken her to the Planetarium and given her a number of excellent books about space, as well as a DVD containing unbelievable photos of 'The Universe' taken from the Hubble space telescope.

Naturally, we all need to attend to the responsibilities of our daily lives, but we also need to remember that we're a part of something more. And if we appreciate our part in this much greater whole, we're likely to be more responsible in the way we relate to all the other people who share this planet Earth.

\* \* \* \* \* \* \* \* \*

### Where All Things Belong        March 2008

About 30 years ago I attended a Conference where a film was shown that changed my perception of the world and everything in it. It was called "Where All Things Belong." It depicted all the ways in which we humans (as well as all of nature) are interconnected and all belong together in this world. It featured many of the ways of thinking of Native Americans who maintained a much closer connection to the earth, to nature, and to the world in general. The film provided many illustrations of the cycles of nature, including the 'cycle of life' by closing with a dramatic scene of a baby being born.

At the conclusion of the film, the hundreds of people in the audience spontaneously stood and cheered. Never had I felt more alive or more connected to others and to the world around

## The Big Picture

me, and I wanted to encourage others to experience this feeling. So we bought a copy of the film and showed it in many of the workshops and seminars we were conducting during those years. Although our old film became no longer useable as technologies changed, its impact has remained with me.

I often think of the film and its concepts these days as I watch the world news and contemplate the tremendous divisions between the various peoples of the world. Despite the globalization brought on by commerce and technology (as well as the universal impact of global warming), we still don't fully appreciate that we're all in this together—regardless of any differences we think may exist between us.

When considering that humans differ from chimpanzees and bonobos by only one per cent of DNA (so close we could accept a blood transfusion or a kidney), we *should* be able to appreciate that humans are 100% linked biologically, in essence being 'the same.' But we continue to act as if anyone unlike us in any way (ethnic, religious, etc.) is somehow 'different.' But our differences are primarily due to our different perceptions based on filtering our view of the world through our own personal experiences.

All too often we fail to cooperate or even *try* to rise above the things that divide us in order to see that what we share in common is far, far greater. In fact, in the long run, we're so interconnected with the rest of the world that if we fail to work for what is best for everyone, we wind up hurting ourselves as well. Only when we open ourselves to the reality that we will all rise together or fall together are we likely to fully embrace the fact that this world is where we *all* belong.

As demonstrated throughout this book, I frequently refer to songs that express ideas I write about. Recently, one particular song has been stuck in my head, so I'll close by sharing part of it.

"We are the World"

*There comes a time*
*When we head a certain call*
*When the world must come together as one*
*There are people dying*
*And it's time to lend a hand to life*
*The greatest gift of all*

*When you're down and out*
*There seems no hope at all*
*But if you just believe*
*There's no way we can fall*
*Well, well, well, well, let us realize*
*That a change will only come*
*When we stand together as one*

*[Chorus]*
*We are the world*
*We are the children*
*We are the ones who make a brighter day*
*So let's start giving*
*There's a choice we're making*
*We're saving our own lives*
*It's true we'll make a better day*
*Just you and me*

\* \* \* \* \* \* \* \* \*

*The Big Picture*

## We're All in this Together                November 2007

If you have regular interactions with a young person between the ages of 6 and 12, you no doubt recognize the above phrase as the central song in the incredibly popular "High School Musical." Since this is a favorite of my granddaughters, I'm quite familiar with it.

While the musical has a positive theme about understanding and embracing differences, this song is sung in such an upbeat way that some might miss the deeper message underneath. However, it's a message the whole world needs to hear—and to implement in ways both large and small.

Here's one of the key verses from the song, exemplifying this larger message:

*"Everyone is special in their own way*
*We make each other strong*
*Were not the same; we're different in a good way*
*Together's where we belong."*

I'm particularly aware of the need for more of this kind of thinking since we've just observed another meeting between Israeli and Palestinian leaders in an effort to address their conflict—which is only one of the many groups of peoples who hold long-standing positions as mortal enemies.

It's tempting to think, 'I can do nothing to change the problem of large groups of people who don't get along.' However, we *can* change the way we handle our own inteactions with people with whom we may have differences, both large and small. We can strive to establish a different, more accepting *attitude* toward others—and pass along this attitude to our children.

As reflected in the song from High School Musical, young people are much more likely to be open-hearted toward others—unless we adults inculcate in them a sense of hatred or mistrust of others who are 'different.' But we won't be able to support this new way of seeing others until we come to a better understanding of how everyone has their own personal view of the world based on their training as children and their personal life experiences.

\* \* \* \* \* \* \* \* \*

**The Whole World**                                               **April 2008**

I'd like to draw your attention to a blinding glimpse of the obvious: the whole world is in trouble, and it's up to us to fix it—especially since much of the mess is of our own making.

Everyone is aware of the problems related to global warming, but that's only the tip of the iceberg, so to speak. All of the many different problems in the world, regardless of whether they're so obviously global, nevertheless affect all of us in some way. So, frankly, we're all in this together—and it will take all of us working together to make it better.

There have been many efforts to mobilize people of the world to come together. One of them is exemplified by the lyrics to a song called "Heal the World."

*Heal the World*
*Make It a Better Place*
*For You and For Me*
*And the Entire Human Race*

*There Are Ways to Get There*
*If You Care Enough for the Living*
*Make a Little Space...Make a Better Place...*
*For You and For Me*

*The Big Picture*

The world's problems are so large and so seemingly insurmountable that it's tempting to think there's nothing you as an individual can do. And we tend to marvel at the stories we hear on the evening newscasts about how some individuals are, in fact, making a difference. But each of us can do *something!* And this is where the power lies—in the accumulation of all the individual efforts we can make.

So let's not sit around waiting and hoping that someone *else* will step forward to take care of these problems. Frankly, that won't happen without the involvement of everyone.

The bottom line is that we're all in this together, and like Lincoln's famous line, *"A house divided against itself cannot stand."* In this case, the 'house' is the Whole World.

www.ingramcontent.com/pod-product-compliance
Lightning Source LLC
Chambersburg PA
CBHW051751040426
42446CB00007B/306